Health Science Fundamentals

Exploring Career Pathways

LAB ACTIVITY MANUAL
TEACHER'S MANUAL

Shirley A. Badasch, M.Ed, RN

Doreen S. Chesebro, B.Ed, LVN

Upper Saddle River, New Jersey 07458

Publisher: Julie Alexander
Publisher's Assistant: Regina Bruno
Executive Editor: Joan Gill
Associate Editor: Bronwen Glowacki
Media Product Manager: John Jordan
Media Project Manager: Stephen Hartner
Marketing Manager: Harper Coles
Marketing Specialist: Michael Sirinides
Marketing Assistant: Lauren Castellano
Senior Managing Editor: Patrick Walsh
Senior Operations Manager: Ilene Sanford
Cover Design: Lissa Auciello-Brogan, Abshier House
Cover Illustration/Photo: Cover images used under license from Shutterstock.com,
    copyright Yuri Arcurs, Doug Stevens, iofoto, Pastushenko Taras, Julián Rovagnati.
Director, Image Resource Center: Melinda Patelli
Manager, Rights and Permissions: Zina Arabia
Manager: Visual Research: Beth Brenzel
Manager, Cover Visual Research & Permissions: Karen Sanatar
Image Permission Coordinator: Kathy Gavilanes
Photo Researcher: Alisa Alering
Composition: Vanessa Moore, Moore Media, Inc.
Project Management and Developmental Editing: Emergent Learning
Editorial Production: Claire Hunter and Michele Somody
Printer/Binder: Courier Printing, Westford, MA
Typeface: 11/14 Minion Pro

Pearson Education Ltd., London
Pearson Education Singapore, Pte. Ltd
Pearson Education, Canada, Inc.
Pearson Education–Japan
Pearson Education, Upper Saddle River, New Jersey

Pearson Education Australia Pty, Limited
Pearson Education North Asia Ltd., Singapore
Pearson Educación de Mexico, S.A. de C.V.
Pearson Education Malaysia, Pte. Ltd.

10 9 8 7 6 5 4 3 2 1

ISBN-13: 978-0-13-504360-8

ISBN-10: 0-13-504360-3

Contents

Scenarios   1

Index of Procedures and Scenarios

Scenarios

Do You Have Time for Me?

You are a health information technician in a busy family practice office. You are in charge of scheduling all office visits. Some of your appointments are by phone, and some are return visits for patients that are already at the office.

Your job is very important because scheduling keeps the day running smooth and patients happy. As busy as people are today, they do not like to be kept waiting. You have to determine the approximate time allotments for each procedure and be sure that you remember when the doctor does special procedures.

Procedure Category	*Schedule Time Needed*
New patient	45 minutes
Routine check-ups	30 minutes
Disease complaints	30 minutes
Office surgical procedure	60 minutes
Office diagnostic test (labs, EKG)	15 minutes

Client's Name	*Reason for visiting doctor*	*Time needed?*
Lori Lieberman	Sore throat	
Misty Buffum	Bloody diarrhea (new patient)	
Doug Pettitti	Excise a skin lesion	
Abdul Halabi	Check-up	
Mollie O'Connell	Upper respiratory infection (new patient)	
Shantiqua Badawi	Pregnancy test	
Karen Winters	Biopsy growth on face	
Theresa Davis	EKG	
Kiku Tamaki	School physical (speaks very little English)	
Manuel Hernandez	Chest pain and trouble breathing	

Things to keep in mind when scheduling patients:

- Your doctor only works until 1230 on Fridays.
- Next Monday is a holiday.
- Next Thursday, from 1400–1500, there is a staff meeting.
- Lunch is from 1230–1400 every day.
- Your doctor only does office surgeries on Wednesdays from 0800–1100.

QUESTIONS TO ANSWER:

- What do you need to be sure to tell each client after you schedule their appointment?
- What is the purpose of tickler cards?
- How would you handle a rude patient that insists he/she see the physician immediately?
- How would you handle patients that were upset because the doctor is running behind due to an emergency and they have been waiting for over an hour?

INSTRUCTOR NOTES:

In this scenario, students have the opportunity to perform the following procedures:

Procedure	Equipment Needed
9.1: Scheduling Office Visits	Pen or pencil
	Appointment book
	Appointment reminder cards for tickler file
	Appointment cards
	Calendar
	Written instructions for patient/client preparation prior to visit
9.2: Scheduling a New Patient/Client: First-Time Visit	Appointment book
	Scheduling guidelines
	Telephone
	Pencil

TEACHING TIPS/STRATEGIES:

Have another student pretend they are calling to make an appointment.

Have another student show up in person to make an appointment.

Make sure that students do not schedule an appointment for the patient having chest pain. He should be instructed to call 911 and get to the Emergency Room.

ADD A TWIST:

Have another patient call who has to be seen immediately because he/she is an emergency and has to be worked into the schedule.

Add a procedure that needs a prep, such as NPO after midnight for certain lab work, Fleet enema, etc.

Be sure the student adds dates on the appointment book.

Tickler cards are an important part of this procedure. Make sure they are used appropriately.

Appointment Book

Time	Monday	Tuesday	Wednesday	Thursday	Friday
0800					
0815					
0830					
0845					
0900					
0915					
0930					
0945					
1000					
1015					
1030					
1045					
1100					
1115					
1130					
1145					
1200					
1215					
1230					

Appointment Book *(continued)*

Time	Monday	Tuesday	Wednesday	Thursday	Friday
1245					
1300					
1315					
1330					
1345					
1400					
1415					
1430					
1445					
1500					
1515					
1530					
1545					
1600					
1615					
1630					
1645					
1700					

Have the student that is scheduling the appointment in person address the below appointment reminder card. On the back of the card, it states "This is a reminder that you have an appointment with Dr. Hopkins on_____ at _____. Please call (000)888-0000 if you need to reschedule."

Hopkins Family Medicine

2 To Test or Not to Test

You currently are employed by a great group of surgeons. They have several medical office assistants on staff, and since each of you are multi-talented, you take turns rotating through the various office positions. This week it is your turn to work in outpatient scheduling.

It is your task to schedule the diagnostic tests that will provide valuable information so that the physicians can treat the patients correctly. Besides needing to be very organized, this job requires strong communication skills.

The patients are often nervous about the tests and what the results may show. You must get them to understand not only when the test will be done, but also any prep that is needed prior to the tests that could affect the results if not done correctly. This task can be challenging.

The first patient to stop by your desk is Charles Conrad. The note from the doctor says you are to schedule Charles for a colonoscopy. Charles is 65 years old and is quite frightened that this test might show he has colon cancer. He has heard some awful things from his friends about how bad the prep can be. He would like to get the colonoscopy done before he leaves on a trip to see his new grandson in two weeks. Please schedule this procedure for Mr. Conrad.

Once you finish with Mr. Conrad, Rosalia Gonzales says she needs your help in scheduling a mammogram. Rosalia is 34 years old and speaks very little English. Her sister died recently from breast cancer, and the doctor has recommended she have this test. She has never had one before. Please schedule this procedure for Mrs. Gonzales.

Reminder to check on test results

Patient Name: _____

Diagnostic Test: _____

Date of Test: _____

Phone Number of Lab or Testing Site:

_____

Date Checked on Test Results: _____

Reminder to check on test results

Patient Name: _____

Diagnostic Test: _____

Date of Test: _____

Phone Number of Lab or Testing Site:

_____

Date Checked on Test Results: _____

QUESTIONS TO ANSWER:

- What could happen if a patient arrived for a procedure and had not carried out the test preparation because you had not given him correct instructions?
- Keeping in mind that many of the patients you are scheduling tests for are frightened about what the outcome might show, how can you make sure they understand your instructions?
- What communication techniques would you use if the patient you were scheduling was deaf?
- What is the function of the tickler cards in this situation?

INSTRUCTOR NOTES:

In this scenario, the student will have the opportunity to perform the following procedure:

Procedure	Equipment Needed
9.3: Scheduling Outpatient Diagnostic Test	Written order from provider
	Test preparation instructions for client/patient

TEACHING TIPS/STRATEGIES:

To make this scenario more realistic, instructors can prepare patient charts for Mr. Conrad and Mrs. Gonzales. Test times are to be recorded in the patient's charts.

Two students can role play these scenarios with one student taking on the role of the person scheduling the procedure and the other student playing the role of the patient.

It is very important for students to review test preparation instructions with the patient both verbally and in writing.

Instructors can go online to the below site and print out colonoscopy instructions, so the students will have written copies to review with the patient.

   http://www.brighamandwomens.org/gastroenterology/ColonPrepPage.aspx

Instructors can go to this site and print out mammogram instructions so the students will have written copies to review with the patient.

   http://www.svmc.net/downloadable_forms/Prep_Instructions_Mammogram.pdf

Copies of tickler cards can be made by the instructor so that they are available for the students to fill out and file. Calendars may also be used.

3   The Aftermath

There is blood everywhere! Blood is pooled in the bed, all over the floor, and there is some even dried on the ceiling. The adrenaline is still flowing and your heart is pumping rapidly. You know you will never be able to sleep tonight. You have just witnessed your first code, and thank goodness the patient survived!

The patient has just been taken to the operating room, and you have been given the task of cleaning up this mess. To make things even more complicated, the charge nurse has just informed you that the patient is HIV positive. There are soiled linens on the bed and multiple contaminated needles on the procedure trays. You are afraid to touch anything.

Once you remove the linens and clean up the equipment, the housekeeping staff will wash down the room. After you finally get the unit cleaned up, you take the dirty procedure trays down to Central Supply. This is the last task you must do before heading home for the night.

Wanda, the Central Supply department chair, is a good friend of your mother and she even gave you a job working in Central Supply last summer. She is so excited to see you. She explains that two of her employees called in sick, and she is really short-handed. There have been three codes tonight and she is running out of clean equipment. She asks if you have a few minutes to clean those dirty instruments and wrap them for autoclave so the hospital will be prepared in case any more emergencies occur during the night. You are exhausted, but you agree to help her.

QUESTIONS TO ANSWER:

- What skills will you need to use to complete these tasks?
- How do you protect yourself from being exposed to the HIV virus when cleaning up the soiled linens and equipment?
- What types of equipment that might have been used in the code would you need to autoclave? Which equipment would you not autoclave?

INSTRUCTOR NOTES:

The chart below shows the order of procedures for this scenario:

Procedure	Equipment Needed
17.1: Hand Hygiene (Washing)	Sink
	Soap
	Paper towels
	Trash can
	Nail brush (if available)
17.2: Personal Protective Equipment	Gown
	Mask
	Nonsterile gloves

Procedure	Equipment Needed
17.7: Transmission-Based Precautions: Applying Personal Protective Equipment	Gown
	Mask
	Nonsterile gloves
17.3: Caring for Soiled Linens	Disposable gloves
	Hamper
17.4: Disposing of Sharps	Disposable gloves
	Sharps container
17.8: Transmission-Based Precautions: Removing Personal Protective Equipment	Mask
	Nonsterile gloves
17.5: Wrap Instruments for Autoclave	Scrub uniform
	Head cover
	Cover gown
	Gloves
	Goggles and/or face mask

TEACHING TIPS/STRATEGIES:

Gowns and gloves should be worn for this scenario. Masks are not needed, as there should not be any splashing.

Linens should be carried away from the body and disposed of appropriately.

All contaminated sharps should be placed in the sharps container.

Personal protective equipment should be removed before leaving the contaminated area and traveling to Central Supply. Make sure students remove equipment correctly to avoid the spread of pathogens.

Goggles and/or face mask should be worn when cleaning instruments for autoclave as splashing and eye exposure could occur.

Make sure autoclave packages are labeled with equipment and date.

4 Protect Your Cranium!

Dakarai, a 20-year-old male, was pumped for the concert. He hopped on his motorcycle and hit the road. The plan was that he would meet all of his buddies at the amphitheater. Because of the high cost of gas he thought driving there on his bike would be a good way to save money.

His mother continued to "be mom" even though he had moved out, and she nagged him about wearing a helmet. Dakarai did not think the helmet looked cool and was glad he lived in a state that did not require head protection. On his way to the concert he accelerated too quickly, lost control, and crashed.

Dakarai suffered severe head trauma, multiple lacerations, and abrasions. When he woke up with a splitting headache, he found himself in a neurological unit and learned that he might not be able to walk again. Just as Dakarai was dealing with learning he may be a paraplegic the rest of his life, you come in to change his sterile dressing on his right shoulder.

Dakarai is abrupt and rude with you, but you know he is on an emotional roller coaster. You also know that you have to remain focused on your task and cannot be rushed so you do not risk contaminating the sterile field. He definitely does not need any more complications.

After you are done changing his dressing you need to get him up in the chair for the afternoon. Dakarai does not want to get up but you encourage him, telling him a change of scenery might make him feel better. Dakarai finally agrees, and you get the Hoyer (mechanical) lift to help you accomplish the task.

QUESTIONS TO ANSWER:

- What do you need to do if you are not sure if you contaminated the sterile field or not?
- What do you need to do if you notice greenish drainage that has an odor when you are changing the dressing?
- What do you need to do if the mechanical lift you go to get is different than the kind you trained on?
- What hospital resources might be available to help Dakarai cope with his diagnosis and make lifestyle adjustments?

INSTRUCTOR NOTES:

In this scenario, students have the opportunity to perform the following procedures:

Procedures	Equipment Needed
17.1: Hand Hygiene (Washing)	Sink
	Soap
	Paper towels
	Trash can
	Nail brush (if available)
17.9: Changing a Sterile Dressing	Nonsterile gloves
	Sterile gloves
	Sterile dressing material
	Tape
	Biohazardous waste container
	A bandage already on a manikin or student acting as the patient
17.6: Putting on Sterile Gloves and Removing Gloves	Sterile gloves (It is a good idea to have various sizes.)
18.29: Transferring—Lifting with a Mechanical Lift	Mechanical lift
	Sheet or blanket for patient comfort
	Sling

TEACHING TIPS/STRATEGIES:

Discuss with students how patients may act angry towards the health care worker often because they are scared or dealing with the unknown. Teaching students not to react, but rather to understand where the patient may be coming from, helps the student be a more effective and empathetic worker.

It is important that standard precautions are maintained throughout the procedures. To see how conscious students are of their sterile field, once they start to put on their sterile gloves, see how they react to someone knocking on the door to come in or to a patient's request to get them water. Do they turn their back on the field? Do they place their hands below their waist? Discuss with them why it is important to be constantly vigilant when dealing with sterile fields so as not to contaminate the field and spread infection.

Discuss with students that throughout any procedure, and particularly the mechanical lift in this situation, it is crucial to explain the procedure to the patient. Ask the student what to do in a situation where a patient refuses the procedure.

If money for supplies is tight, try getting outdated sterile dressing supplies from a local health care facility. If reusing sterile gloves/dressings must be done between students, be sure to put the gloves/dressings back in the package exactly as they come and have students simulate opening the package as if it was not already open. Discuss with students how to check if the sterile equipment being used is still in date.

5 School Provides Free Sports Physicals

The athletic trainer has recruited your health sciences class to help with the sport physicals for the upcoming football season. You and a few other students have been recruited due to your interest in sports medicine.

During the physical exam, the students will be responsible for gathering the following information: vital signs, height, weight, and vision. They will be doing the physicals in the school gym.

The coaches have a scale, but you will need to bring the rest of the equipment you need from the classroom. You will need to complete the form on the following page for each athlete before they see the physician.

Sports Physical Form

Name: _____ Date: _____ Sport: _____

Address: _____

Birthday: _____ Allergies: _____

Medications: _____

Vital Signs:

Oral Temperature: _____ °C

Radial Pulse: _____

Apical Pulse: _____

Respirations: _____

Blood Pressure: _____

Height and Weight:

Height: _____ feet/inches

Weight: _____ pounds

Vision Test:

Right eye: _____ Left eye: _____

Corrective Lenses: _____

QUESTIONS TO ANSWER:

- What equipment do you need to bring to the gym?
- How can you ensure privacy for your patients in a school gym?
- You take an athlete's blood pressure and it is very high. He is very nervous. What do you do?
- The team's star athlete has an irregular pulse and very high blood pressure. If you write this on the form, he might not get to play and could lose his chance for scholarships. What do you do?

INSTRUCTOR NOTES:

The chart below shows the order of procedures for this scenario:

Procedure	Equipment Needed
17.1: Hand Hygiene (Washing)	Sink
	Soap
	Paper towels
	Trash can
	Nail brush (if available)
18.2: Measuring an Oral Temperature Using a Mercury or Nonmercury Thermometer	Clean oral thermometer
	Alcohol wipes
	Watch with a second hand
	Disposable thermometer cover
18.6: Counting a Radial Pulse	Watch with a second hand
	Pad and pen
18.7: Counting an Apical Pulse	Stethoscope
	Alcohol wipes
18.8: Counting Respirations	Watch with a second hand
	Pad and pen
18.9: Palpating a Blood Pressure	Sphygmomanometer
18.10: Measuring Blood Pressure	Alcohol wipes
	Stethoscope
	Sphygmomanometer
	Pad and pen
20.2: Measuring Weight on a Standing Balance Scale	Portable balance scale
	Paper towels
	Paper and pen

Procedure	Equipment Needed
20.5: Measuring Height	Balance scale with height rod
	Paper towels
	Paper and pen
20.6: Measuring Height of Adult/Child (over 3 years of age)	Balance scale with height rod
	Paper towels
	Paper and pen
20.19: Testing Visual Acuity: Snellen Chart	Snellen charts
	Occluders
	Pointers
	Measuring tape

TEACHING TIPS/STRATEGIES:

Students should provide privacy for the patient and explain each procedure before they do them.

Have both the red and blue probes out for the electric thermometers and make sure students choose the blue probe for oral temperatures. Students need to dispose of probes correctly after taking the temperature. Students need to convert the Fahrenheit temperature to Celsius.

Occasionally, tell a student that an athlete has an irregular radial pulse and see if they take it for one full minute rather than 30 seconds.

Ask students what they would do if an athlete comes in with a very high blood pressure (have the athlete relax for 5 to 10 minutes and retake the pressure). If still high, document it and report it to the physician.

Students should clean the stethoscope bell and diaphragm between each athlete, as well as wash their hands. Students should note rate, rhythm, and strength of the apical pulse.

New paper towels should be placed on the scales before each athlete is weighed.

The balance bar should be raised before the athlete steps up on the scale, and they should be instructed to face away from the scale when their height is measured.

If the athlete has corrective lenses, his vision needs to be checked with and without the lenses.

SCENARIO 6 — Does Baby Benjamin Measure Up?

You have been looking forward to this clinical experience for a long time. You love working with children, and you have dreams of working in pediatrics after graduation. Today you are going to be working in a free pediatric clinic at a local community hospital.

Your first patient is a 6-month-old baby boy, named Benjamin. His mother has brought him in for his check-up. Benjamin is not a happy boy. He is scared of you and starts to scream. You note on his chart that the doctor wants you to get vital signs, height and weight, and measure his head circumference.

Benjamin also needs a urine specimen to be collected and tested this visit. You tell his mother to remove his clothes so you can get his height and weight, and you leave the room to gather your equipment. When you return, Benjamin is still fully clothed and still crying. Once again you ask his mother to remove his clothes so you can get an accurate weight. Benjamin's mother continues to cuddle her son, but does not begin to remove his clothes.

You notice that she is talking to him in Spanish. You suddenly realize that she does not speak English. How will you handle this challenging situation?

QUESTIONS TO ANSWER:

- How will you communicate with the mother that does not speak English about the exam?
- If you do not have an infant scale, how can you weigh the patient?
- What alternative modes of measuring body temperature could you use if your clinic did not have an aural thermometer?
- Why are apical pulses taken on infants?
- Why should an infant not be crying when you count respirations?

INSTRUCTOR NOTES:

The chart below shows the order of procedures for this scenario:

Procedure	Equipment Needed
17.1: Hand Hygiene (Washing)	Sink
	Soap
	Paper towels
	Trash can
	Nail brush (if available)
20.9: Measuring the Weight of an Infant/Toddler	Infant balance scale
	Towel
	Growth chart
	Clean towel
	Pen and paper
20.8: Measuring the Height of an Infant/Toddler	Tape measure
	Pen and paper
	Exam paper or sheet (optional)
20.7: Measuring the Head Circumference of an Infant/Toddler	Measuring tape
	Pen and paper
20.28: Collecting Urine from an Infant	Specimen container
	Disposable urine collector
	Disposable nonsterile gloves
18.5: Measuring an Aural (or Tympanic) Temperature	Aural thermometer
	Disposable probe covers
	Pen and paper
18.7: Measuring an Apical Pulse	Stethoscope
	Alcohol wipes
	Pen and paper
18.8: Counting Respirations	Watch with second hand
	Pen and paper

TEACHING TIPS/STRATEGIES:

Communication is a challenge because the mother does not speak English. (If the student speaks Spanish, change the mother's language to Russian or French.) Students will have to use nonverbal communication skills.

Students should put the disposable urine collector on while the baby is undressed, and they can check it at the end of the exam.

Have several types of thermometers to choose from such as an electric thermometer with an oral probe, an aural thermometer, and a glass oral thermometer. Students need to choose which type of thermometer would be best for infants.

Students need to make sure the child has stopped crying before counting respirations so the count will be accurate.

Height, weight, and head circumference need to be charted on a growth graph. Students also need to note that an aural temperature was obtained.

ADD A TWIST:

The clinic does not have an aural thermometer or an infant scale. How can students complete the exam?

No aural thermometer? Students can do an axillary or rectal temperature—Procedure 18.4: Measuring an Axillary Temperature OR Procedure 18.3 Measuring a Rectal Temperature.

No infant scale? The student can weigh the mother and then weigh mother and baby. After this they subtract the mother's weight to get the baby's weight.

7 Good Morning Roger

You have been assigned to work on the rehabilitation unit today. Your first patient is an 82-year-old gentleman named Roger. Roger had a stroke two weeks ago that left him very weak on the right side. He is right-handed, so he gets frustrated very easily.

He also has very poor vision and has been declared "legally blind." He lost his vision due to his diabetes. Roger wears dentures on the top, but has been able to keep his own teeth on the bottom. It is policy that all patients on the rehabilitation unit must be dressed in loose clothing and out of bed, sitting in their wheelchairs for breakfast. You do not need to worry about Roger's bath, as this has been done by the 3–11 shift.

Your assignment is to assist Roger with the above tasks, as well as with his breakfast, so he will not be late for his morning therapy session. Roger is very independent and wants to feed himself, he just needs some assistance. Roger also asks you for a special favor. He knows you are busy, but he has not had a shave in two days, and his whiskers are getting pretty scratchy.

QUESTIONS TO ANSWER:

- What skills do you need to perform and in what order should they be done?
- Since Roger is visually impaired but wants to feed himself, how can you help him remember where the food is located on his tray?
- Which side of the body will you undress first and why? Which side of the body will you dress first?

INSTRUCTOR NOTES:

In this scenario, students are to perform the following procedures:

Procedure	Equipment Needed
17.1: Hand Hygiene (Washing)	Sink
	Soap
	Paper towels
	Trash can
	Nail brush (if available)

Procedure	Equipment Needed
18.11: AM Care	Washcloth and towel
	Toothbrush and toothpaste
	Emesis basin
	Glass of water
	Denture cup
	Clean gown
	Comb and brush
	Disposable gloves
18.21: Offering the Urinal	Urinal with cover
	Soap and water
	Towel and washcloth
	Disposable nonsterile gloves
18.15: Oral Hygiene—Self Care	Toothbrush and toothpaste
	Mouthwash
	Cup of water with straw, if needed
	Emesis basin
	Bath towel
	Tissues
18.18: Oral Hygiene—Denture Care	Tissues
	Paper towel or gauze squares
	Mouthwash
	Disposable denture cup
	Toothbrush or denture brush
	Denture paste or toothpowder
	Towel
	Disposable nonsterile gloves
	Emesis basin
18.53: Shaving the Patient	Electric shaver or safety razor
	Shaving lather or an electric preshave lotion
	Basin of warm water
	Face towel
	Mirror
	Aftershave
	Disposable gloves
	Balloon (optional if having students shave balloons)

Procedure	Equipment Needed
18.59: Preparing a Patient to Eat	Bedpan or urinal
	Toilet tissue
	Washcloth
	Hand towel
18.61: Assisting the Patient with Meals	Patient's ID band
	Dinner menu
	Food tray with food, drinks, straws, silverware
	Over-bed table
18.25: Pivot Transfer from Bed to Wheelchair	Bed
	Wheelchair
	Patient footwear
	Gait belt (if used)

TEACHING TIPS/STRATEGIES:

Have several different types of clothing for students to choose from when dressing the patient.

A student posing as the patient should have on a gown or pajamas and needs to have an ID bracelet on.

The patient has right-sided weakness, so students need to take soiled clothes off the unaffected (left) side first and put clean clothes on the weak (right) side second.

Balloons can be blown up and a face drawn on them. Students can practice shaving the balloon if you do not want them to shave another student. If the balloon pops, they cut the patient.

Prepare several food trays which represent different diets for different patients. One could have sugar free Jell-O and a diet drink for the diabetic. A regular diet could have some pudding, cereal, etc. It is a good idea to find something for each tray which has to be cut up for the patient. Make sure they have drinks, silverware, napkins, and straws. You can pick up extra seasonings like salt and pepper at fast-food restaurants.

Students need to check the patient's name band with the name on food tray.

The patient has very poor vision, so the clock method should be used when describing the location of food on the tray. Review feeding patients with disabilities.

Lights Out

It has been a busy evening, but things are starting to settle down. The halls are free of visitors, and most of the patients are in their rooms watching TV and resting. It is time to offer bedtime snacks, provide fresh drinking water, and help folks settle down for a good night's rest.

Your first task is to serve nourishments. You have several diabetics on the floor, and they need some crackers and milk before bed. Once snacks are served, you begin your rounds to tuck your patients in for the night.

Your first patient is Lucy Long. Lucy slipped on a banana in the grocery store and broke her left hip four days ago. She is 75 years old and her skin is paper thin. She is the perfect candidate to develop a decubitus ulcer, and she refuses to move off her back.

You offer Lucy a back rub if she will allow you to position her on her side for a couple of hours. She agrees and you examine her skin while performing the back rub. So far, so good and no skin breakdown or redness is noted. You position Lucy on her side and hope she will fall asleep before she rolls back on her back again.

Finally you stop in to see Tim McDonald. Tim recently lost his right leg in an accident at work. Tim is sitting in the wheelchair and needs assistance in getting back to bed. He needs to be lifted into bed, so you call another nurse to help you.

You also need to place the bed cradle back on the bed, as Tim cannot stand the weight of the sheets on his fresh stump. After getting Tim in bed and chatting with Tim for about 10 minutes, you make sure all the patients have fresh water for the night. You dim the lights in the hall and wish them all sweet dreams.

QUESTIONS TO ANSWER:

- What skills do you need to be able to perform to settle these folks in for the night?
- Why can laying on your back for prolonged periods of time lead to the formation of decubitus ulcers?
- What type of nourishments would be appropriate for a diabetic patient? A heart patient? A patient on a clear liquid diet?

INSTRUCTOR NOTES:

The chart below shows the order of procedures for this scenario:

Procedure	Equipment Needed
17.1: Hand Hygiene (Washing)	Sink
	Soap
	Paper towels
	Trash can
	Nail brush (if available)
18.65: Serving Nourishments	Nourishment
	Cup, dish, straw, spoon
	Napkin
18.12: PM Care	Washcloth and towel
	Toothpaste and toothbrush
	Glass of water
	Emesis basin
	Night clothes
	Lotion
	Linen as needed
	Disposable gloves
18.36: Turning Patient on Side	Bed
	Pillows
18.13: Skin Care—Giving a Back Rub	Lotion
	Powder
	Towel
	Washcloth
	Soap
	Water
	Bath thermometer
	Disposable gloves
18.27: Transferring—Two Person Lift from Bed to Chair and Back	Chair
	Bed
18.58: Placing a Bed Cradle	Bed cradle
18.63: Providing Fresh Drinking Water	Water pitcher
	Cup

TEACHING TIPS/STRATEGIES:

The instructor can have several different types of nourishments available as well as the names of different patients and their ordered diet. Students will need to check the diet order before delivering nourishments. For example, you would not want to give a regular soda and ice cream to a diabetic.

Instructors can also add calculating and recording intake on I&O sheets to this scenario.

Good body mechanics should be used with PM care, turning the patient on their side, and the two person lift. Check to see that students are raising and lowering the bed when appropriate.

The bedside table and call bells should always be placed within the patient's reach before leaving the room.

Condition of the skin should be noted and documented both when giving back rubs and when turning the patient. The instructor can add to the scenario by telling the student that the patient has evidence of skin breakdown at certain bony prominences and check to see if they react appropriately.

Wheels of both the bed and wheelchair need to be locked before lifting a patient from the chair to the bed. Make sure students check these before proceeding with the lift.

Charts can be created for patients on the unit. Diagnosis and diet orders can be included in these charts as well as orders for fluid restriction. Students can discuss why patients might be placed on fluid restriction and problem solve if they should be served fresh water.

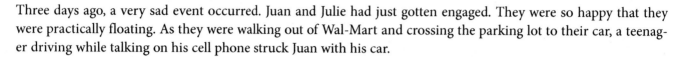

I Can Still Hear You

Three days ago, a very sad event occurred. Juan and Julie had just gotten engaged. They were so happy that they were practically floating. As they were walking out of Wal-Mart and crossing the parking lot to their car, a teenager driving while talking on his cell phone struck Juan with his car.

As Juan lay on the ground bleeding and unconscious, Julie screamed and covered him with her body as if to shield him from any further danger. This could not be happening. Juan was airlifted to the hospital and remains in the Neuro ICU with massive head trauma. He is still unconscious. Julie has not left the hospital since he was admitted. Juan is your patient today.

You have been assigned to bathe Juan, give him mouth care, and make his bed. You ask Julie if she would wait outside in the waiting room while you complete AM care on Juan. Julie asks if you could please wash his hair and change his gown. He still has dried blood in his hair, and she knows he would not want everyone staring at his dirty hair.

Juan is also on nasal oxygen and has been breathing through his mouth. He has IV fluids running into his right arm. He has a Foley catheter, and your instructor reminds you to be very careful when doing his catheter care.

QUESTIONS TO ANSWER:

- In what order would you complete these skills to be the most efficient with your time?
- Why do you turn the patient's head to the side when doing oral care?
- Why would you need to explain what you were doing to an unconscious patient who does not respond to your voice?
- What complication could occur if the catheter was left kinked?

INSTRUCTOR NOTES:

The chart below shows the order of procedures for this scenario:

Procedure	Equipment Needed
17.1: Hand Hygiene (Washing)	Sink
	Soap
	Nail brush (if available)
	Paper towels
	Trash can

Procedure	Equipment Needed
18.19: Oral Hygiene—for the Unconscious Patient	Emesis basin
	Towel
	Lemon glycerin swabs
	Tongue blades
	4 × 4 gauze
	Lip moisturizer
	Gloves
18.43: Giving a Bath	Soap and soap dish
	Face towel
	2–3 Bath towels
	2–3 wash cloths
	Clean hospital gown
	Bath blanket
	Lotion or powder
	Nailbrush & emery board
	Comb & brush
	Bedpan or urinal & cover
	Bed linen
	Bath basin
	Bath thermometer
	Disposable nonsterile gloves
18.71: Giving Indwelling Catheter Care	Antiseptic solution or catheter care kits
	Waterproof bed protector
	Disposable nonsterile gloves
	Bath blanket

Procedure	Equipment Needed
18.48: Shampoo the Hair in Bed	Chair
	Basin of water
	Pitcher of water
	Bath thermometer
	Paper or styrofoam cup
	Large basin
	Shampoo tray or plastic sheet
	Waterproof bed protector
	Pillow with waterproof cover
	Bath towels
	Small towel
	Cotton balls
18.46: Patient Gown Change	Clean patient gown
	Disposable nonsterile gloves
18.56: Making an Occupied Bed	Disposable nonsterile gloves
	Draw sheet or large pad
	Two large sheets or fitted bottom sheet and one large sheet
	Two pillowcases
	Blankets as needed
	Bedspread (if a clean one is needed)
	Pillow

TEACHING TIPS/STRATEGIES:

This scenario works best with one student taking on the role of the patient and one student taking on the role of the health care worker.

Explain to students that research has shown that even though patients are unconscious, many still possess the sense of hearing and also respond to touch. It is important that students talk to the patient and tell them what they are going to do before they do it.

Hospitals will often donate IV fluids that are out of date. To make the scenario more realistic, have fluids attached to IV tubing and tape the tubing to the patient.

Body mechanics and safety issues are very important in this scenario. Students need to raise the bed up to do mouth care and bathing the patient. In turn, they need to remember to lower the bed when they are finished. They need to remember to pull side rails up when they are making an occupied bed.

Patient privacy needs to be protected while doing these procedures. Privacy screens or curtains should be pulled and patients should not be exposed. The bath blanket helps protect privacy as well as keep the patient warm.

When doing mouth care on the unconscious patient, make sure the student turns their head to the side to avoid aspiration.

Disposable equipment used in mouth care needs to be put in hazardous waste containers due to the exposure to body fluids.

Emphasize the need to assess the condition of the skin when bathing and turning the patient.

Make sure students test the water temperature before bathing the patient and before washing their hair. Students should check the water during the bath and change water if it becomes too cool in temperature.

Instructors can tell the student if Juan is circumcised or uncircumcised.

Students need to make sure that the catheter is not kinked and not pulling when they finish their procedure.

ADD A TWIST:

It would be appropriate to add the following procedures to this scenario, as these tasks are usually carried out in this situation:

- Procedure 19.6: Elastic Hose (Antiembolism Hose)

  and

- Procedure 19.4: Range of Motion

10 Granny Doesn't Know Me Anymore

One of the sad things about Alzheimer's disease is that individuals eventually forget basic skills such as hygiene, how to feed themselves, and toilet training. Often as the disease progresses, these patients will need to be placed in an extended care facility.

That is where you have been assigned to work today—the Alzheimer's unit in a local nursing home. You will be taking care of Frieda, a 78-year-old female who is in the late stages of Alzheimer's disease. She does not talk much and does not remember how to walk. It is almost like taking care of a large infant.

This is Thursday, and it is Frieda's day to get a shower, nail care, and shampoo. Due to her inactivity and poor eating habits, she has a terrible constipation problem. Frieda has not had a bowel movement in the past five days, so the doctor has also ordered a soap suds enema for her today.

All of these tasks need to be completed between breakfast and her art therapy at 10:30. While she is in art therapy, you can get her bed made. The shower room is down the hall and to the right. Make sure you have all your supplies as you cannot leave Frieda alone in the shower room. What supplies will you need? In what order will you accomplish these tasks?

QUESTIONS TO ANSWER:

- What communication techniques would you use if Frieda becomes agitated and will not cooperate with you during her care?
- How can you maintain Frieda's privacy when she is naked in the shower?
- What will you do if the patient experiences cramping during the enema?
- If Frieda cannot use the bedpan, how will you handle the outcome of the enema?

INSTRUCTOR NOTES:

The chart below shows the order of procedures for this scenario:

Procedure	Equipment Needed
17.1: Hand Hygiene (Washing)	Sink
	Soap
	Paper towels
	Trash can
	Nail brush (if available)
20.17: Left Lateral Position and Left Sims Position	Bed
	Sheet

Procedure	Equipment Needed
18.69: Tap Water, Soap Suds, Saline Enemas	Disposable gloves
	Disposable enema equipment:
	Plastic container
	Tubing
	Clamp
	Lubricant
	Enema soap solution
	Bath thermometer
	Bedpan and cover
	Urinal, if necessary
	Toilet tissue
	Waterproof disposable bed protector
	Paper towel
	Bath blanket
18.20: Elimination—Offering the Bedpan	Bedpan with cover
	Toilet tissue
	Soap and water
	Towel and washcloth
	Disposable gloves
18.31: Transferring—Moving a Patient to a Wheelchair	Wheelchair
18.45: Tub/Shower Bath	Bath towels
	Washcloths
	Soap
	Bath thermometer
	Wash basin
	Clean gown
	Bath mat
	Disinfectant solution
	Shower chair

Procedure	Equipment Needed
18.49: Shampooing in Shower or Tub	Shampoo
	Washcloth
	Towel
	Cream rinse, if desired
	Cotton balls
	Hairdryer
18.46: Patient Gown Change	Clean gown
	Disposable gloves
18.50: Arranging the Hair	Comb and/or brush
	Towel
18.51: Nail Care	Bath basin with warm water
	Orange sticks
	Emery board
	Nail clippers
	Disposable gloves
18.57: Making an Open Bed	Disposable gloves
	Draw sheet or large pad
	Two sheets or fitted bottom sheet and one large sheet
	Pillowcase
	Blankets as needed
	Bedspread (if a clean one is needed)
	Pillow

TEACHING TIPS/STRATEGIES:

The order of procedures is very important in this scenario. Students need to realize that they need to give the enema before they bathe the patient.

It is also important to gather all the equipment they will need as they must continue to supervise the patient.

Communication is important with Alzheimer's patients. Students need to explain each procedure before doing it so the patient will not be frightened.

Make sure students use good body mechanics by raising and lowering the bed during the enema and when transferring patient to the wheelchair.

Privacy is important and patients should be covered at all times except for when they are in the shower. Privacy curtains should be pulled when available.

Water temperature should be tested both before the shower and before nail care.

During the enema, tell the student the patient is experiencing cramping. Students should clamp tubing for a minute and lower the bag.

Cotton balls should be placed in the patient's ears before washing their hair and removed when shampoo is completed.

Patient needs to be dry and in a clean gown before hair is dried. Patients may need to be wrapped in a dry blanket if they are chilled.

Hairstyle should be age appropriate.

All procedures and results of care should be documented correctly.

Some facilities require that you have a doctor's order before trimming nails.

11 The Flip-Flop Trip Up

Going out the door to get a pedicure done, Marie realized she forgot her book to read. Turning to get her book, Marie's flip-flops got tangled and she fell, hitting the bed and landing on a wooden floor. Marie broke her sacrum in two places and her pelvis in two places.

She has recently returned home from the hospital, but has physical therapy coming to her house three times a week. You have been assigned to work with Marie today. When you read her chart, you see they have been working with Marie on getting out of bed and walking with a walker.

Today you are also going to help her learn how to walk with a cane. She is to put most of her weight on the right side. She is very frightened of falling and weak after several weeks of bed rest. When you finish ambulating the patient, you are to apply ice to her sacrum for 15 minutes to decrease edema and pain.

QUESTIONS TO ANSWER:

- What equipment will you need to bring to Marie's home to carry out these tasks?

- How will you deal with Marie's fright about falling again and encourage her to learn a new procedure?

- Marie argues she needs to hold the cane in her left hand since that is the weaker side. Why does she need to hold the cane in her right hand?

- Why do you need to assess a patient's skin after ice has been applied to it?

INSTRUCTOR NOTES:

In this scenario, students are to perform procedures in the following order:

Procedure	Equipment Needed
17.1: Hand Hygiene (Washing)	Sink
	Soap
	Paper towels
	Trash can
	Nail brush (if available)
18.24: Assist to Dangle Stand and Walk	Bed
	Patient's footwear
	Gait belt (if used)
19.7: Ambulating with a Gait Belt	Gait belt
	Patient's robe
	Patient's footwear
19.10: Ambulating with a Walker	Walker in good condition
	Patient's footwear
	Patient's robe
19.8: Walking with a Cane	Cane in good repair with rubber tip
	Patient's footwear
	Patient's robe
	Dry cryotherapy: Ice
	Bags/ice collars
	Ice bag or commercial cold compress
	Ice
	Cover for ice bag

TEACHING TIPS/STRATEGIES:

Students should instruct the patient to hold the cane in her right hand. They also should tell her to move the cane and her weakest foot (left) forward at the same time.

Students should make sure the metal cap of the ice bag does not touch the skin. They should also check skin color and position of the bag frequently.

Students need to document how the patient tolerated the procedures.

Home Sweet Home

Today you are working as a nursing assistant on a medical-surgical unit. As you return to the med-surg unit after lunch, Diane, the unit secretary, tells you that the physician has been in and discharged Mr. Binkie.

His wife is on the way to pick him up, and she will be here in about 20 minutes. Mr. Binkie is a 28-year-old male who has been in the hospital for 5 days with a staph infection. He had been snorkeling in the Caribbean and rubbed against some coral. When he returned home, his arm had become red, swollen, and sore. He was admitted to the hospital and put on IV antibiotics.

You know he will be excited to be going home, as he has missed his children and complains he cannot get any rest at the hospital due to people checking on him every hour. Mr. Binkie is in a semi-private room, and to make things worse, his roommate snores very loudly.

When you go in to see how close he is to being ready to go home, you note that he still has his IV connected, and he says the nurse has not been in to go over his prescriptions yet. He asks you, "How can I get my valuables back that were sent to the cashier's office?" You assure him that you will get those things for him.

Mr. Binkie insists he can walk to the car, but you explain it is hospital policy that all patients must be escorted out in a wheelchair. Your task is to discharge Mr. Binkie and then return to the unit.

The housekeeping staff has finished cleaning his bed when you return, and you need to make a closed bed so the room will be ready for the next patient that needs it.

QUESTIONS TO ANSWER:

- Which tasks are within your scope of practice as a nursing assistant and which are not?
- What do you need to do if some of the patient's valuables are missing?
- What will you do if Mr. Binkie tries to give you a cash tip when you take him to the car?
- Why do you make a closed bed when you return versus an open bed?

INSTRUCTOR NOTES:

The chart below shows the order of procedures students have the opportunity to perform:

Procedure	Equipment Needed
17.1: Hand Hygiene (Washing)	Sink
	Soap
	Nail brush (if available)
	Paper towels
	Trash can
20.11: Discharging the Patient	Pt. belongings & valuables
	Admission list
	Wheelchair
18.30: Transferring—Moving a Patient in a Wheelchair	Wheelchair
18.55: Making a Closed Bed	Bed
	Fitted bottom sheet and one large sheet
	Draw sheet or large pad
	Blankets as needed
	Bedspread
	Pillow
	Pillowcase

TEACHING TIPS/STRATEGIES:

Put together a zip-lock bag or envelope that has valuables in it. This could include a man's wallet, an old watch, a ring, some pill bottles with M&Ms in it, etc.

Have a chart made up for Mr. Binkie that includes a discharge order, some discharge prescriptions, nurses' notes, and an admission form that was completed earlier. Students need to return the valuables to the patient and check them with the admission form. If you wanted to make this more challenging, you could have something missing from the bag with valuables and see how the student reacts.

Hospitals will often donate IV fluids that are out of date. To make the scenario more realistic, have fluids attached to IV tubing and tape the tubing to the patient.

Privacy needs to be provided for the patient during the discharge procedure.

The nursing assistant cannot remove the IV or review medications with a patient. This needs to be done by a nurse.

Good body mechanics need to be used while making the bed. Bed should be raised and lowered at appropriate times.

One side of the bed should be completely made before the going to the other side of the bed.

Linens should not be pulled back.

13 | I Can't Get Up

Abby Sullivan is a 73-year-old female who is recovering from the heart bypass surgery she had yesterday. She is still in the ICU, and she is on a ventilator. She also has an external pacemaker, chest tubes, central line, and multiple IVs.

Abby's surgery went well, but she is having an adverse reaction to some of the medications. Abby is very agitated and confused. She has tried to get out of bed, and she has tried to pull out several of her tubes. She has actually pulled her IV out twice.

Her family has gone home for the night to get some much needed rest, so there is no one out in the waiting room who can stay with her. You contact her surgeon who gives you an order to use restraints if needed. You decide they are definitely needed, as you are afraid for her safety.

You have two major goals to accomplish with these restraints. One is to keep her in bed so she does not fall and fracture any bones, and the other one is to keep her from pulling out all of her tubes.

QUESTIONS TO ANSWER:

- Which type(s) of restraints do you need to apply?
- What extra care will the patient need when you use them?
- What alternatives could you use in place of restraints?

INSTRUCTOR NOTES:

The chart below shows the order of procedures students have the opportunity to perform:

Procedure	Equipment Needed
17.1: Hand Hygiene (Washing)	Sink
	Soap
	Nail brush (if available)
	Paper towels
	Trash can
18.38: Applying Restraints	Doctor's order for restraints
	Restraints
18.39: How to Tie Postural Supports	Vest postural support
18.41: Postural Supports: Mitten	Soft cloth mitten
18.42: Postural Supports: Vest or Jacket	Developed X-rays
	X-ray mounts
	View box

Procedure	Equipment Needed
19.4: Range of Motion	Sheet or blanket
	Treatment table or bed
	Good lighting

TEACHING TIPS/STRATEGIES:

Have students come up with a list of alternative measures they could try before applying restraints.

Health care workers must have a physician order's order before applying restraints, and it must be renewed every 24 hours. One option with this scenario is to have an order, but the date and time on the order obtained is greater than 24 hours. Does the student notice this, and if so, what do they do?

Family members need to be notified when restraints are applied and the reasons for this action.

The restrained extremity needs to remain in normal anatomical position. Arms should not be restrained above the head, etc.

Knots should be easily released by pulling the end of the loop. Once the restraint is applied and tied, the instructor could change the scenario by announcing there is a gas leak, and you must evacuate the unit. How fast can the restraint be untied?

Circulation and skin condition under the restraints needs to be checked every 15–30 minutes and documented on the progress notes.

Tell the students 2 hours have passed. Restraints should be removed for 10–15 minutes and range of motion exercises done. This also should be documented.

Review False Imprisonment law and resident rights under Omnibus Budget Reconciliation Act.

ADD A TWIST:

Have students use limb postural supports instead of mitten postural supports.

- Procedure 18.40 Postural Supports: Limb

14 Midday Meal Time

Lunch has just arrived on the unit and, as a nursing assistant, one of your assigned tasks is to help pass out meal trays and assist with feeding patients when needed. All of your patients can feed themselves except for Abdul Smith.

Mr. Smith, an 82-year-old male, has had a right BKA (below the knee amputation) due to diabetes and also has some upper extremity weakness.

After you help the rest of your patients get started with their lunch, you go to Mr. Smith's room to prepare him for his meal. Before eating, Mr. Smith tells you he "needs to micturate." When you go to remove the urinal, you notice he has slipped down in the bed and his left foot is hanging off the end of the bed.

You assist Mr. Smith with repositioning and then with eating his meal. When he is through with lunch, he asks if you could please clean his dentures as his family is coming to visit in an hour, and he does not want food stuck in his teeth.

QUESTIONS TO ANSWER:

- What procedures do you need to do and in what order?
- Why is it important to reposition Mr. Smith before assisting with feeding?
- What complications could occur if Mr. Smith gets a tray that does not have a diabetic diet on it?

INSTRUCTOR NOTES:

In this scenario, students have the opportunity to perform the following procedures:

Procedure	Equipment Needed
17.1: Hand Hygiene (Washing)	Sink
	Soap
	Paper towels
	Trash can
	Nail brush (if available)
18.21: Elimination—Offering the Urinal	Urinal with cover
	Soap and water
	Towel and washcloth
	Disposable nonsterile gloves
18.33: Moving—Assisting Patient to Sit Up in Bed	Bed
	Pillows

Procedure	Equipment Needed
18.61: Assisting the Patient with Meals	Patient ID band
	Dinner menu
	Food tray with food, drinks, straws, silverware
	Over-bed table
18.18 Oral Hygiene—Denture Care	Tissues
	Paper towel or gauze squares
	Mouthwash
	Disposable denture cup
	Toothbrush or denture brush
	Denture paste or toothpowder
	Towel
	Disposable nonsterile gloves
	Emesis basin

Note: Procedure 17.1: Hand Hygiene (Washing) must be used throughout.

TEACHING TIPS/STRATEGIES:

Since Mr. Smith has upper extremity weakness, you can adjust how much help Mr. Smith needs with the urinal. Have students describe why they need to observe the patient's urine and what normal versus abnormal is. To make the situation more realistic, put simulated urine or apple juice in the urinal.

Question the students on different ways to move the patient up in bed (i.e., with patient assistance if able, with a coworker, with a lift). Ask the students what position you need to put the patient in to eat in bed (Fowlers) and why this position is needed (to help prevent aspiration). Students need to use good body mechanics and be sure to lock the wheels on the bed before moving the patient.

Have a tray prepared that has food and beverages the students can feed the patient. Remember to include silverware, straws, and items that need to be opened.

Be sure the student articulates/performs/simulates matching meal ticket with patient ID bracelet. Make sure the student feeds the patient at a slow pace and asks the patient what they would like to be served.

ADD A TWIST:

Have the patient be on Intake and Output. Have students record intake and output and ask them to name conditions why a person would need to have this monitored.

Add red food coloring to the urine to simulate hematuria. Ask students what to do in this situation and what conditions may cause hematuria.

SCENARIO

15 | To Do or Not to Do—That Is the Question

Matt, a physical therapy assistant student, is training with you in the physical therapy department today. You introduce Matt to the first patient on the schedule today, Kathy Pearson. Ms. Pearson, a new resident at Shady Brook Estates, is struggling with limited movement.

To help prevent contractures and to help increase her mobility, Ms. Pearson's physician has written the following order: ROM qod by PT. You ask Matt if he would like to perform Ms. Pearson's range of motion exercises today.

You also mention to Matt that Mr. Pearson is very hard of hearing. Matt, still in training, has not learned how to perform these exercises yet, but is afraid to admit that to you.

QUESTIONS TO ANSWER:

- What should Matt do?
- How do ROM exercises help prevent contractures?
- How do you respond when asked to do things beyond your scope of practice?
- How can you communicate with patients that are hard of hearing?

INSTRUCTOR NOTES:

In this scenario, the student will have the opportunity to perform the following procedures:

Procedures	Equipment Needed
17.1: Hand Hygiene (Washing)	Sink
	Soap
	Paper towels
	Trash can
	Nail brush (if available)
19.4: Range of Motion	Sheet or blanket
	Treatment table or bed
	Good lighting

TEACHING TIPS/STRATEGIES:

The student should perform the ROM, since Matt is not trained. Have students discuss why they should not do something they have not been trained to do. Ask students what they should do if they are asked to do something not covered in their training (i.e. give medicines).

Review with students the importance of reporting any pain that the patient expresses.

Invite a physical therapy assistant and/or a physical therapist to come and be a guest speaker for the class. Ask him/her to demonstrate range-of-motion exercises and talk about strategies to prevent contractures.

ADD A TWIST:

Have this procedure done with some active and some passive ROM.

Victory Comes Crashing Down

As Bobby waited in the exam room, he thought back to the track meet yesterday. He kept replaying the moment in his head. He pictured himself reaching for the baton being passed to him. The handoff was done with absolute precision.

He knew his team was in the lead and their time had to be the fastest they had posted all season. As Bobby rounded the last turn and the finish line was in his sight, he felt his ankle turn and twist. Bobby crashed to the ground and the team's hopes of a victory crashed with him.

In slow motion, he could see the baton flying off the track and landing with a thud in the grass. How could this have happened! All of the team's hours of practice in the heat was for naught, and there was only one more meet this season.

His ankle was sprained, and he was not sure if his teammates would ever forgive him. Instead of participating in a victory celebration, he was here waiting to have his ankle wrapped and get crutches. Your job is to provide Bobby with care for his sprained ankle and instruction for walking with crutches.

QUESTIONS TO ANSWER:

- What complications can occur if crutches are not fitted properly to the patient?
- Why is wrapping the ankle the treatment of choice? What other treatment is used?
- What other situations might require a joint to be wrapped or taped?

INSTRUCTOR NOTES:

In this scenario, students have the opportunity to perform the following procedures:

Procedure	Equipment Needed
17.1: Hand Hygiene (Washing)	Sink
	Soap
	Paper towels
	Trash can
	Nail brush (if available)
21.20: How to Care for a Sprain	
19.5: Wrapping/Taping an Ankle	Ace bandage
19.9: Walking with Crutches	Crutches

TEACHING TIPS/STRATEGIES:

Have students explain why it is important to be sure they do not wrap the ankle too tightly. How do they assess this?

Have students compare strains and sprains and the treatment for both.

- Procedure 21.19: How to Care for a Strain

Have students name other joints that can be supported by tape and elastic bandages (i.e., elbow, wrist, and shoulder).

Invite an athletic trainer to be a guest speaker in your class. Have him/her demonstrate how to wrap a joint.

The Perfect Host/Hostess

As a medical assistant, you are responsible for patient admissions. You are often the first person with whom the patient comes in contact with and you need to help the patient feel comfortable.

Today you welcome a new patient, Mr. Wong. Mr. Wong is a 44-year-old male admitted to the unit with acute gastroenteritis. There are no family members with him. His wife has gone to the beach for a weekend with her girlfriends, and she is driving back but will not be here for about 3 more hours.

Mr. Wong is wearing shorts, a football T-shirt, and sandals. Mr. Wong has brought his medicine from home: Synthroid 137 mcg, Actos 30 mg, and Diovan HCT tab 80/12.5. Mr. Wong is allergic to shellfish. It makes his mouth and tongue swell. He wears bifocals and is proud to report he still has all of his teeth. He has a gold necklace, a watch, and a gold wedding band. His wallet has $55 in cash and 3 credit cards.

He was in the hospital twice before. When he was 24, he got hit in the jaw with a baseball and had to have his jaw wired. When he was 32, he had a little problem with kidney stones and had to have lithotripsy.

His main concern is how to turn on the television because there is a football game starting in 15 minutes that he cannot miss.

You know you must make careful observations and notify the nurse immediately if there are any acute problems. As you develop your rapport with Mr. Wong, you fill out the admission checklist form, orient him to the room, and gather baseline information on the patient.

QUESTIONS TO ANSWER:

- How can you make the patient feel at ease?
- What acute problems might you encounter during admission?
- What are your legal responsibilities related to Mr. Wong's belongings?
- When his wife arrives, what information can your share with her and what information is protected by the HIPAA Law?

INSTRUCTOR NOTES:

In this scenario, students have the opportunity to perform the following procedure:

Procedure	Equipment Needed
20.1: Admitting a Patient	Admission checklist
	Admission pack
	Bedpan
	Urinal
	Emesis basin
	Wash basin
	Tissues
	Sink
	Soap
	Paper towels
	Trash can
	Nail brush (if available)
	Gown or pajamas
	Portable scale
	Thermometer
	BP Cuff
	Stethoscope
	Clothing list
	Envelope for valuables
	"Valuables"
	Urine specimen collection equipment (optional)
	Armband

TEACHING TIPS/STRATEGIES:

This procedure encompasses other procedures as well—hand washing, making an open bed, height and weight, TPR and BP, and urine specimen collection. Depending on time, past skill checkoffs, etc. you may want the student to just articulate some of these skills.

To help students with communication skills, have a second student act as the patient. These patients need to have an arm band on to be checked by the professional admitting the patient.

Have patients be different ages and cultures; have different disabilities (i.e., blindness, hard of hearing); and have some acute issues (i.e., respiratory distress).

Make sure to encourage students to smile as they introduce themselves to help the patient feel at ease.

Remind students that they must be professional, observant, and friendly. Trying to make the patient feel at ease is important, and it is critical that the information obtained is as accurate as possible.

This scenario lends itself to additional skills as well. For instance, if the patient has hemiplegia, they would need assistance with dressing and transferring to the bed. The patient might have a seizure or heart attack while being admitted.

Discuss what adaptations can be taken if the patient is deaf, blind, incontinent, etc.

Patient rights and responsibilities can be discussed.

18 Dip to Diagnose

As a Medical Assistant, you love your job because no two days are the same and the job never gets boring. You get to do various tasks that help the physician in determining a diagnosis for the patient. A diagnosis is the first step in making the patient feel better.

You call your first patient of the day, Mabeline O'Malley, to come back to the exam room. Mabeline is a 33-year-old female who is eight months pregnant with triplets. She is in a wheelchair because she tripped over her toddler's toys and broke her right tibia.

As she comes back to the exam room, you ask how she has been feeling. Since she is having multiple babies, the doctor is watching her closely for gestational diabetes and toxemia.

The first thing you do is get her weight; a large increase in pounds and swelling could be a sign of toxemia. Since she can't stand, you will have to weigh her in the wheelchair.

Next you instruct her on how to obtain a midstream clean-catch urine. You offer to assist her, but Mrs. O'Malley says she can handle it. When Mrs. O'Malley brings you the urine specimen, you test the urine using a reagent strip, looking for signs of glucose and protein.

You continue to be fascinated by the information you can obtain with the urine test dipstick. You document the results of the test on her progress notes. As the doctor comes in, you wish Mrs. O'Malley good luck in case the babies come before you see her again. You consult the schedule and go to call your next patient.

QUESTIONS TO ANSWER:

- What would you do if you did not note the time you started the dipstick test? (Would it make a difference?)
- How would you get the patient's weight if you did not have a chair scale in your office?

INSTRUCTOR NOTES:

In this scenario, students need to perform the following procedures:

Procedure	Equipment Needed
20.3: Measuring Weight on a Chair Scale	Portable balance scale
	Paper towel
	Paper and pen
20.26: Midstream Clean-Catch Urine, Female	Sterile urine container
	Label
	Disposable antiseptic towelettes
	Disposable nonsterile gloves
20.22: Urine Reagent Strips to Test Urine	Reagent strips and bottle
	Laboratory report slip
	Watch
	Urine specimen
	Disposable nonsterile gloves

TEACHING TIPS/STRATEGIES:

Since handwashing needs to be used for the above procedures, you can incorporate that into the skills that students need to do for check off—Procedure 17.1: Hand Hygiene (Washing).

Ask the students to describe other ways in which patients are weighed (standing balance scale, mechanical lift, baby scale).

Simulated urine that will have various lab results can be purchased from many medical or biological suppliers. Apple juice can also be used as simulated urine and will test positive for glucose. Ask the student why a clean-catch method is used. (To prevent possible specimen contamination.)

Be sure students check the expiration date on the reagent jar. Discuss with students why it is important to do this. Have students come up with reasons a person's urine might be tested in this manner and what the results could indicate.

Be sure students read the reagent strip at the accurate time. Have students explain why this is important.

If you have the equipment, you may have the student measure the specific gravity with a urinometer or refractometer.

- Procedure 20.23: Measuring Specific Gravity with Urinometer

   OR

- Procedure 20.24: Measuring Specific Gravity with Refractometer

19 Assume the Position

Though it is early in the morning, the sun is shining, and it is already quite warm outside as you unlock the office door. It would be a great day to play golf or lie by the pool, but the general practitioner you work for has a full schedule today.

The first thing you do is turn on the computer and print out the patient appointments for the day. As a medical assistant, it is your responsibility to greet the patients and prepare them for the doctor's exam or procedure. This involves placing them in the right position.

Below is a copy of the day's schedule, which includes the patient's name and procedure being done. Position each patient as they arrive, so the doctor can be efficient in carrying out the treatments and procedures she must do today and not get behind schedule.

Time	Name	Procedure
9:00–9:30	Ed Bath	Drainage of Abscess on Left Buttock
9:31–10:00	Myrtle Gomaz	Pap Smear
10:01–10:45	Peter Cheng	Proctoscope Exam
10:46–11:20	Pierre deMontfort	Rectal Exam and Oil Retention Enema
11:30–1:00	Lunch	
1:00–1:30	Ariella Lieberman	Breast Exam
1:31–2:15	Marcella Mancini	Severe Hypotension, (Goes into shock while in the office)
2:25–3:00	Chuck Brown	Abdominal Pain
3:01–3:45	Gretel Braun	COPD and Chest Pain
3:46–4:15	Bob Beamer	Hemorrhoids
4:16–5:00	Geevan Patel	Insert Foley Catheter

QUESTIONS TO ANSWER:

- What alternative exam position could you place a patient in if they had hemorrhoids and were pregnant?
- How would you handle an elderly patient that was very modest and did not feel comfortable removing their clothes and putting on a patient gown?
- In which exam positions should you not leave the patient unattended and why?

INSTRUCTOR NOTES:

Some procedures or treatments might have multiple positions that would be appropriate. If you want them to use a particular position, you may need to give them some additional information about the patients such as "they are recovering from abdominal surgery" or "they are pregnant."

PROCEDURES AND POSITIONS:

Drainage of Abscess on Buttock—20.16: Prone Position

Pap Smear—20.15: Dorsal Lithotomy Position

Proctoscoope Exam—20.18: Knee-Chest Position

Rectal Exam & Oil Retention Enema—20.17: Left Lateral Position and Left Sims' Position

Breast Exam—20.12: Horizontal Recumbent (Supine) Position

Severe Hypotension—20.14: Trendelenburg Position

Abdominal Pains—20.12: Horizontal Recumbent (Supine) Position

COPD & Chest Pain—20.13: Fowler's Position

Hemorrhoids—20.18: Knee-Chest Position

Insert Foley Catheter—20.15: Dorsal Lithotomy Position

20 Habits Can Be Deadly

Susan is waiting to see the gerontologist. She hates going to the doctor and is very anxious about this appointment. To calm her nerves, she moves into the corner of the room and sneaks a cigarette. She knows she should not smoke for various health reasons, but cannot seem to break her bad habit.

As she lights up her cigarette, her portable oxygen tank sparks a fire. Your coworker tends to Susan who has second degree burns on her face and chest. After ensuring the rest of the clients in the waiting room are safe, you focus on the rack of magazines which have caught on fire.

After putting the fire out you think the emergency is over, but suddenly Pedro, another client in the waiting room, grabs his chest and collapses from what appears to be a cardiac arrest. He does not have a pulse and is not breathing. Was the stress of the fire too much for him?

QUESTIONS TO ANSWER:

- How do you put out the fire?
- What does your coworker do to treat Susan's burns?
- How do you respond to the client that has collapsed?
- What would you need to do if the fire got out of control and you cannot extinguish it?

INSTRUCTOR NOTES:

In this scenario, students have the opportunity to perform the following procedures:

Procedure	Equipment Needed
21.1: How to Operate a Fire Extinguisher	Fire extinguisher
21.11: Treating Burns	Disposable gloves
	A way to stop the burning process
	Dry, sterile nonstick dressing
21.22: Cardiopulmonary Resuscitation-Adult	Disposable gloves
	Pocket mask or bag mask
21.25: Demonstrating the Use of AED (Automated External Defibrillator)	AED Trainer

TEACHING STRATEGIES/TIPS:

Ask the students to name the three elements that must be present for a fire (oxygen, heat, and fuel) and explain why someone who is on oxygen should not smoke.

Have several types of fire extinguishers or signs representing fire extinguishers available and have the students choose which one they would use for this type of fire. Later, let the students explain their choice of fire extinguisher. Have students explain what "PASS" means (Pull the pin, Aim at the base of the fire, Squeeze the handle, and Sweep back and forth).

Students must know to monitor burns of the face and upper torso very closely for breathing problems. Also, since shock is a possibility, students must treat patients appropriately until EMS arrives.

This scenario may be done with two students—have one student treat the burns and the other do CPR. A third student can assist with CPR (Procedure 21.23: Performing CPR, Two Person). Be sure the student has a coworker call 911 and get the AED.

Be sure students use standard precautions throughout the procedures.

Often your local fire department will come to the school and light controlled fires for students to practice using a fire extinguisher.

ADD A TWIST:

Have the pretend fire get out of control and have the students problem solve what they need to do (remove the clients from immediate danger).

Suggest that Pedro has a hairy chest and the AED pads are not able to stick to it (in this case the student would rip off the pads to remove the hair or use a razor if supplied in the AED case).

Have someone throw water on the fire, so that when Pedro collapses he is wet and laying in a large puddle of water (in this case Pedro would have to be dried off and moved out of the water before administering a shock).

21 Action at the Eatery

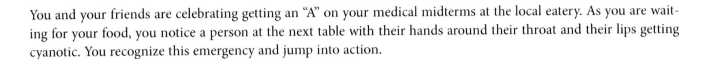

You and your friends are celebrating getting an "A" on your medical midterms at the local eatery. As you are waiting for your food, you notice a person at the next table with their hands around their throat and their lips getting cyanotic. You recognize this emergency and jump into action.

QUESTIONS TO ANSWER:

- What is the medical emergency?
- What do you do if the person refuses your assistance?
- How do you determine if the person is just "playing around?"
- How would the rescue procedure change if the victim weighed 350 pounds?
- What would you do if the patient loses consciousness?

INSTRUCTOR NOTES:

In this scenario, students have the opportunity to perform the following procedure:

Procedure	Equipment Needed
21.3 Obstructed Airway in a Conscious Victim—Adult	A choking victim

TEACHING TIPS/STRATEGIES:

Make sure the student asks the victim if they are choking and identifies themselves while asking for permission to help. Remind students to position themselves so as to have good balance if the victim goes unconscious (i.e., one of their legs between the victim's legs, so they can help ease the victim down if they loose consciousness).

Review with students what to do in the case of an obese or pregnant victim.

To check this procedure off as a class, have one half of the students (those simulating choking) stand and face the other half. It is quick and easy to check off students in line. Be sure students know that they are NOT to perform real abdominal thrusts on a person who is not choking BEFORE they start this procedure!

Choking manikins can be purchased from many medical suppliers; these give students the opportunity to fully practice this skill.

ADD A TWIST:

Have the victim say they are choking and be sure the student knows that they are not choking if they can talk.

Have the victim be coughing and be sure the student knows to encourage coughing and to stay with the victim until they are better.

Have the victim become unconscious and follow the guidelines for Procedure 21.4: Obstructed Airway in an Unconscious Victim—Adult.

22 4th of July Gone Awry

It is a beautiful day. There is not a cloud in the sky, and you are happy to have the day off so you can enjoy the holiday. You are attending a neighborhood 4th of July party.

Everyone is enjoying "pigging out" on hotdogs and hamburgers, and playing Frisbee and volleyball. Suddenly, you hear a woman scream, "My baby, my baby! Somebody help my baby!"

You scan the crowd and see a woman picking up her baby who must have fallen face down in the baby pool when the mother was not looking. The baby's body is limp and unresponsive. The baby's lips are turning blue, and she has a bluish-grey color to her complexion. You have just been certified in infant CPR and go to render assistance while another guest calls 911.

QUESTIONS TO ANSWER:

- What do you do?
- Would you handle this situation differently if you were alone?
- What other circumstances might cause an infant to stop breathing?

INSTRUCTOR NOTES:

In this scenario, students have the opportunity to perform the following procedures:

Procedure	Equipment Needed
21.24: Cardiopulmonary Resuscitation—Infant	Barrier devices: Nonsterile gloves Infant-sized barrier device for ventilations
Procedure 21.5: Stopped Breathing in an Infant (optional procedure for modified scenarios)	Barrier devices: Nonsterile gloves Infant-sized barrier device for ventilations

TEACHING TIPS/STRATEGIES:

Since handwashing needs to be done after the above procedures, you can incorporate that into the skills students need to do for check off:

- Procedure 17.1: Hand Hygiene (Washing)

In any emergency situation, it is important to stay calm. Ask students in what ways they can make this happen.

In any procedure dealing with possible blood or body fluids, it is important to maintain standard precautions. Ask the students how to handle this situation if they do not have barrier devices.

Go over the Good Samaritan Law as it pertains to your state with the students.

ADD A TWIST:

Have the infant only needing rescue breathing.

Have the infant need rescue breathing. After the student rechecks breathing and pulse, state that the infant is now without a pulse. Students need to be sure to check the brachial artery. This twist ensures that the student does know she needs to continue to monitor the infant's pulse.

Have a second rescuer help with infant CPR.

Have the student be alone babysitting and get distracted by talking to their boyfriend/girlfriend on the phone. Discuss the differences in when to call 911 when doing CPR on infants and children versus adult CPR.

The Lost Lego Legend

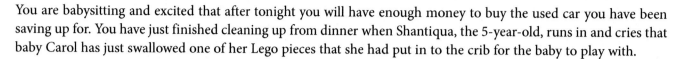

You are babysitting and excited that after tonight you will have enough money to buy the used car you have been saving up for. You have just finished cleaning up from dinner when Shantiqua, the 5-year-old, runs in and cries that baby Carol has just swallowed one of her Lego pieces that she had put in to the crib for the baby to play with.

You hear the high pitched sounds of the baby's cry as she struggles to get any air exchange. Her little lips are turning blue. Your adrenaline kicks into high gear. You rush over to baby Carol's crib, swoop her up, and begin trying to release the Lego.

QUESTIONS TO ANSWER:

- What procedure do you do?
- How can you tell if a baby is choking or not since they will not use the universal sign of the hands around the throat?
- What would you do if the infant becomes unconscious?

INSTRUCTOR NOTES:

In this scenario, students have the opportunity to perform the following procedure:

Procedure	Equipment Needed
21.6: Obstructed Airway in a Conscious Infant	Disposable gloves
	Baby manikin

TEACHING TIPS/STRATEGIES:

Students need to recognize what to do in this medical emergency. Ask them how to tell if a baby is choking or not, since they will not use the universal sign of the hands around the throat.

To help expedite checking off this skill, if you are able to have enough manikins for a couple of students, conduct this skill as a group with everyone practicing the skill at the same time.

Ask the students how they would feel in this situation. If any students have had to do this procedure in real life, ask them if they would like to share their experience.

Ask the students what to do once the airway is no longer obstructed.

Have a guest speaker from your local EMS discuss home emergencies and how to handle them.

ADD A TWIST:

Have baby Carol go unconscious—Procedure 21.7: Obstructed Airway in an Unconscious Infant.

24   When Seconds Count

You are driving home from teaching first aid to a troop of Girl Scouts. You are singing with the radio and wondering if you should try out for the next *American Idol* when you pass by a car that has crashed into a tree and is in a ditch. You pull over and rush to see if everyone is all right.

As you get out of your car, you smell burnt rubber and hear cries for help. As you survey the scene, you see one passenger sitting on the side of the road moaning as a fountain of blood spurts out from her left lower arm.

A second victim is standing next to the car. She is alert and oriented, but holding her right arm, which is hanging from her elbow at a strange angle. As you take a closer look, you suspect the bone is fractured, but it has not pierced the skin.

A passerby stops and asks if there is anything he can do to help. He says he "does not have first aid training, but he is a quick study." You have the first aid supplies that you used in the class in the trunk of your car.

QUESTIONS TO ANSWER:

- Which supplies will you need?
- What do you need to do and in what order?
- What do you have the passerby do?
- How will you know if one of the victims is going into shock?

INSTRUCTOR NOTES:

In this scenario, students have the opportunity to perform the following procedures:

Procedure	Equipment Needed
21.15: Circular Bandaging of a Small Arm Wound	Disposable gloves 4 × 4 gauze pads Gauze roll
21.8: Preventing Shock	Blanket Something to elevate legs
21.12: Applying a Splint	Disposable gloves Firm object for splint Roller gauze
21.13: Applying a Triangular Sling	Disposable gloves Material in the shape of a triangle for a sling

TEACHING TIPS/STRATEGIES:

Students must be able to assess a situation and perform basic triage. Make sure students survey the scene and ensure that it is safe for them to approach before they do any patient care. They can have the passerby call 911, direct traffic, help the victims remain calm, etc.

The students must first attend to the medical emergency of bleeding. They need to use standard precautions. Have the student come up with barriers they can use if they do not have gloves. Since it is an arterial bleed, the student must note that basic pressure and elevation will probably not be sufficient, and the brachial artery must be used. Once the bleeding is controlled and the arm is bandaged, the student must recognize that shock is a concern due to the loss of blood.

To make this seem more realistic, use a moulage kit that has spurting blood. Also you can make a wound with the moulage kit or you can make a wound using household items. To make your own wound, mix together petroleum jelly, red food coloring, and cocoa powder. Place this mixture on the skin and add small pieces of single ply tissue to add texture to the wound.

After caring for the bleeding patient, students can apply a splint and sling to the broken arm. The student must realize that this victim also may go into shock and must monitor and treat appropriately.

Invite a local EMT or paramedic to speak when doing this scenario in class.

ADD A TWIST:

Have the second victim with a broken leg and make sure the rescuer does not raise that leg to prevent shock.

25 Sticks and Stones Will Break Your Bones

Terrie Thomas, a 26-year-old male, was out riding an ATV (all terrain vehicle/ "4 wheeler") with his friends. While racing up a steep hill, his vehicle suddenly flipped over. Terrie was lucky to jump off so as to not have the vehicle land on him.

He heard, as well as felt a loud snap as his arm landed on a rock. He suffered a mild concussion and a simple fracture of his right radius, which needed a closed reduction to repair it. The orthopedist reduced the fracture, then applied a cast to immobilize the break. It was a painful procedure, as he could not sedate Terrie due to the concussion.

The doctor told him he was lucky to have survived with only a broken arm and to have avoided needing surgery. He told Terrie that he would like to admit him overnight due to his concussion.

Terrie has been admitted to your unit for observation. After getting him settled into his room, you complete his neurological checks and get ready to perform his cast care.

QUESTIONS TO ANSWER:

- What do you need to check for?
- Why is it important to elevate the extremity above the patient's heart level?
- What could malodor from the cast indicate?

INSTRUCTOR NOTES:

In this scenario, students have the opportunity to perform the following procedure:

Procedure	Equipment Needed
21.21: Cast Care	Pillows for positioning

TEACHING TIPS/STRATEGIES:

Have students share past experiences (personal or other) with broken bones and casts. Have students share how they felt immediately after the break, a day after the break, and two weeks after the break.

To make the scenario more realistic, have X-rays available which show the fracture. Have students determine the type of fracture and the bone that is fractured. You can often get x-rays from radiology centers or orthopedics to use in class.

As students assess distal circulation, ask them what to do if the patient has on fingernail polish.

If you decide the patient has a plaster (vs. fiberglass) cast, ask students why the patient must be repositioned every 2 hours for 24–48 hours after the cast is applied.

Review with students the need to instruct patients not to use hangers, etc., if they have an itch under the cast.

Invite an orthopedist or a physician's assistant to speak to the class. Sometimes they will actually put a cast on one or more of the students.

26 Pearly Whites

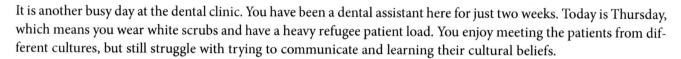

It is another busy day at the dental clinic. You have been a dental assistant here for just two weeks. Today is Thursday, which means you wear white scrubs and have a heavy refugee patient load. You enjoy meeting the patients from different cultures, but still struggle with trying to communicate and learning their cultural beliefs.

Your first patient, Jace Lim, is in for a cleaning and X-rays. When your patient sits in the dental chair, you catch a whiff of his breath and you are overcome with nausea. Your patient's halitosis is overwhelming.

Mr. Lim is a refugee from Cambodia, and he speaks limited English. When he first looks at you and your uniform, his expression suddenly changes from a smile to one of fright.

You remember from your training that you must watch your nonverbal expressions, maintain professionalism at all time and use tact. This is one of those situations your instructor warned you about—one in which maintaining professionalism might not be easy.

You have 30 minutes to brush and floss his teeth and determine how to best communicate to Mr. Lim the importance of proper oral hygiene. X-rays will be taken by the dental hygienist, and after they are developed, you need to properly mount them.

QUESTIONS TO ANSWER:

- With respect to his culture, why might Mr. Lim be frightened when he sees you?
- How do you handle this situation with respect to his culture?
- What is a tactful way to handle his halitosis?
- How do you make sure your patient understands your instructions?

INSTRUCTOR NOTES:

In this scenario, students have the opportunity to perform the following procedures:

Procedure	Equipment Needed
17.1: Hand Hygiene (Washing)	Sink
	Soap
	Paper towels
	Trash can
	Nail brush (if available)
17.2: Personal Protective Equipment	Nonsterile gloves
	Mask
	Goggles

Procedure	Equipment Needed
22.1: Bass Toothbrushing Technique	Toothbrush
	PPE
22.2: Dental Flossing	Dental floss
	PPE
22.3: Mounting Dental Films	Developed X-rays
	X-ray mounts
	View box

TEACHING TIPS/STRATEGIES:

Be sure students include proper nutrition as a way to help prevent periodontal infection and disease.

Ask students why it is increasingly important for healthcare workers to be able to communicate with people of different cultures and understand their beliefs and rituals.

A tooth model with toothbrush may be used as a model for teaching.

Having the patient gargle with mouthwash before working on them is sometimes standard procedure and would be a way to tactfully help handle the halitosis.

Note that the patient from Cambodia might be frightened when he sees the dental assistant in all white because of cultural differences: White is a sign of bad luck and indicates mourning and death.

ADD A TWIST:

Change the patient's age and have student count the patient's teeth (there are 32 permanent teeth in dentition and 20 deciduous teeth in dentition), noting how many are missing.

Have students identify different types of teeth and parts of the teeth as a review.

Have a tray with different dental tools on it and have the students identify what the tools are and what they are used for.

If you have a local refugee office or international office, set up a speaker to come in and share information about different cultures and common dental practices of different countries.

Contact a local community college to see if one of their dental assistant teachers and/or students would speak to the class.

Don't Turn Your Back!

"Hey hon!" your mom calls from the den when you walk in the door from school. She introduces you to a friend of hers, Mrs. Fedak, who is visiting. Mrs. Fedak has her 2½-year-old daughter, Isabel, with her. Isabel is cute as a button and Mrs. Fedak explains that Isabel is quite a handful, and she is at the age where she likes to get into everything!

After exchanging pleasantries, you head to your room. You put your book bag down and know you have to get your chores and homework done before you can go out. It's your turn to clean the bathrooms, so you get to work. While you are cleaning, you are jamming to your iPod, drowning out the sound of the world around you.

You have had quite a day. It started with a pop quiz in physics and just went downhill from there. Thank goodness there was a substitute in history.

You are just about done with the first bathroom, and as you stand back to admire the sparkling sink and mirror, you turn around and see Isabel drinking the bottle of cleaner! What do you do?

QUESTIONS TO ANSWER:

- What could you have done to prevent this accident?
- What complications could occur from this poisoning?
- Why don't you just read the label of the cleaner to see what to do if the cleaner is ingested instead of calling poison control?
- Why might poison control ask for the age and weight of the victim?

INSTRUCTOR NOTES:

In this scenario, students have the opportunity to perform the following procedures:

Procedure	Equipment Needed
21.9: Treating a Conscious Poison Victim	Disposable gloves
	Empty cleaning agent bottle
	Poison control number

TEACHING TIPS/STRATEGIES:

The national poison control number is 1-800-222-1222. Be sure students know this number as well as their state poison control center number.

Be sure the students know to be alert for shock or respiratory problems when dealing with poisonings.

Discuss with students the proper storage of cleaning supplies (in their original containers and locked out of toddlers' reach).

Talk about other types of poisons and how you would treat them with students.

Review with students that if they are babysitting or in charge of small children, it is a good idea to know the child's age and weight, as well as allergies and any medical conditions. Emergency numbers for reaching parents, doctors, and EMS are also important to have handy.

For an extension activity, have students research online about poison prevention and make a bulletin board for the school.

ADD A TWIST:

Change the type of poison that is ingested to pills or have it be an insect or snake bite. Have the student problem solve what to do differently. Have students discuss what to do if a person inhaled a poison and how to protect themselves.

Have the victim go into shock or have breathing problems.

Have the victim be unconscious—Procedure 21.10: Treating an Unconscious Poison Victim.

28 Black Diamond Disaster

You are on a ski retreat in the mountains with some friends. On your way up the ski lift, the cool air chills your exposed face and the snow is gently falling on the ground. It is a perfect day for skiing, and so far the beginner and intermediate slopes have been a blast.

As you and your friend, Manuel, get off the lift you wobble a little bit, but then regain your balance. You both decide to try the expert black diamond slope this time. After all, how hard can it be?

Neither of you will admit the fear you feel as you look at the incline of the slope, nor will either of you admit that this slope might be too advanced. You egg each other on, and then go for it.

Your buddy teases you that you've actually spent most of the time going down on your gluteus maximus, but you feel a rush as you consider you have successfully navigated your way halfway down the mountain. You've even worked up enough courage to try going over the moguls or bumps. As you continue down the slope, your speed becomes harder and harder to control. You fly over a mogul, go sailing in the air, and then "wham!"

You land hard on your shoulder and you continue to slide down the hill. As you come to a stop, your head hits a rock. You remain conscious, but are in agonizing pain. You know you've dislocated your shoulder and feel blood running down the back of your head. Manuel, who was not far behind, can't stop in time and swerves to avoid you and lands in the woods. During the fall, his right leg slams into a briar patch causing a large wound on his thigh. On top of that, his left foot came out of the boot and a sharp broken tree branch sliced his foot. How will ski patrol handle your injuries?

QUESTIONS TO ANSWER:

- Should ski patrol suspect a back or neck injury? If so, what should they be sure to do?
- What purpose does a dressing serve?
- Why don't you remove a dressing once it has been applied?
- What complications could possibly occur from these injuries?

INSTRUCTOR NOTES:

The following procedures are pertinent for this scenario:

Procedure	Equipment Needed
17.1: Hand Hygiene (Washing)	Sink
	Soap
	Paper towels
	Trash can
	Nail brush (if available)
21.14: Triangular Bandaging of an Open Head Wound	Disposable gloves
	Gauze pad
	Triangular bandage
21.16: Spiral Bandaging of an Large Wound	Disposable gloves
	Wound dressing
	3–6 inches of gauze roll
	Medical tape (optional)
21.17: Bandaging of an Ankle or Foot Wound	Disposable gloves
	Wound dressing
	1–2 inches of gauze roll
21.18: How to Care for a Dislocation	Immobilization device
	Ice

TEACHING TIPS/STRATEGIES:

Have two students act as the victims and two students act as the rescuers. Standard precautions must be maintained throughout this scenario.

Discuss with students how to ensure that the scene is safe and the rescuers and victims stay out of harm's way.

Have the rescuer discuss procedures that occur in the hospital for the dislocation.

Have students share experiences they may have had with any of the above injuries.

Have students discuss how they would feel if they were in this situation.

Have students explain how they would monitor and treat complications that could occur.

ADD A TWIST:

Have one of the skiers break an arm—Procedure 21.12: Applying a splint and Procedure 21.13: Applying a Triangular Sling.

Have one of the skiers sprain an ankle—Procedure 21.20: How to Care for a Sprain.

Moving Day

You are the nurse for Dino Pappas today. Dino is a pleasant 54-year-old man who is paralyzed from the waist down due to a gunshot wound five years ago. He is in the hospital due to exacerbation of his emphysema. He is glad to be moving from his current semi-private room to a private room. His roommate and his roommate's visitors have been very loud and inconsiderate. Mr. Pappas states he has not even been able to watch his favorite TV shows!

Mr. Pappas had received some Tylenol earlier as he was running a fever, and you first must see if his fever has gone down. You grab the electronic thermometer, take his temperature, and note that he is afebrile.

As you are gathering his medications and belongings, the respiratory therapist walks in and wants to assess his pulmonary function and administer his breathing treatment before he is transferred. As the RT finishes up, he connects Mr. Pappas' oxygen via nasal canula to the portable oxygen tank, so Mr. Pappas is ready for transfer. You slide him from the bed to the wheelchair, secure his oxygen tank, and wheel him and his belongings to his new room.

When Mr. Pappas arrives in his private room, he is thrilled. You make sure you put away all of his belongings and help him back in bed. You position him on his right side, using the logrolling technique as he turns on his favorite show, *The Price is Right*!

QUESTIONS TO ANSWER:

- What is your role in assisting/promoting respiratory therapy?
- What pulmonary techniques might Mr. Pappas need?
- How often should Mr. Pappas change position? Why is this important?
- How would you handle the roommate conflict, if transferring the patient was not an option?

INSTRUCTOR NOTES:

The following procedures are pertinent for this scenario:

Procedure	Equipment Needed
17.1: Hand Hygiene (Washing)	Sink
	Soap
	Paper towels
	Trash can
	Nail brush (if available)
18.1: Using an Electronic Thermometer	Plastic thermometer cover/sheath
	Electronic thermometer with appropriate probe
19.11: Respiratory Therapy	Props if available: oxygen tank, nasal canula
18.26: Transferring—Sliding from Bed to Wheelchair and Back	Wheelchair with removable arms
20.10: Moving Patient and Belongings to Another Room	Patient's chart
	Nursing care plan
	Medications
	Paper bag
18.34: Logrolling	Bed
	Pillows

TEACHING TIPS/STRATEGIES:

Students need to be sure the wheels on the bed and wheelchair are locked before transferring. Proper body mechanics must be maintained. When the patient is put back in bed, it is important that proper body alignment is maintained.

Discuss with the student how their role would be different if they were a nursing assistant instead of a nurse (i.e., they could not transfer medications).

Have students discuss what to do in situations where roommates don't get along.

Review pursed lip breathing with students; discuss why this technique helps someone with emphysema.

Invite a respiratory therapist into class to discuss pulmonary function.

30   Spin Cycle

You have been working in the lab for just over a year now. Working here gives you great satisfaction, as you know your role is crucial in detecting and diagnosing diseases. This doctor's office keeps you on your toes and brings a variety of different tests each day.

As you wait for your first patient, you make sure all of your supplies are stocked. As you look up, Mr. Liam Curtis arrives and hands you his lab orders. You see that you will need to centrifuge his urine and look at it under a microscope as well as measure the specific gravity with a refractometer.

He states he has been having some problems with his urination, and "the doctor is checking on his kidneys." You explain to him how to obtain a midstream clean-catch urine specimen and that when he is done, he is to bring the specimen back to you. When he returns, you thank him and get to work.

QUESTIONS TO ANSWER:

- What can you learn from centrifuging urine and from looking at it under the microscope?
- What other tests might the doctor order?
- What time of day is the ideal time to obtain a urine specimen for centrifuging?

INSTRUCTOR NOTES:

The following procedures are pertinent for this scenario:

Procedure	Equipment Needed
20.27: Midstream Clean-Catch Urine, Male	Sterile container for clean catch
	Label
	Disposable antiseptic towelettes
	Disposable nonsterile gloves
20.25: Centrifuging a Urine Specimen	Centrifuge
	Two centrifuge tubes
	Microscope slide (number slide)
	Coverslips
	Pipette
	Disposable nonsterile gloves
	Urine specimen

Procedure	Equipment Needed
20.24: Measuring Specific Gravity with Refractometer	Disposable gloves
	Refractometer
	Distilled water
	Fresh urine sample
	Eye dropper or pipette
20.21: Using a Microscope	Microscope
	Lens paper
	Slides and slide covers
	Specimen
	Disposable nonsterile gloves

TEACHING TIPS/STRATEGIES:

Fake urine can be purchased at a number of medical suppliers.

Standard precautions must be maintained throughout the procedures.

Urine must not be overspun, as some elements may form clumps and cause unevenly distributed slides. Review with students why the first morning specimen is the specimen of choice for centrifuging.

Have students research different medical diseases/disorders where urine testing is a diagnostic tool.

Discuss with students why a clean-catch collection is done.

Be sure to demonstrate how to use a centrifuge, refractometer, and microscope before students use them.

If your classroom does not have a centrifuge, see if you can take a field trip to a lab. Perhaps you can invite a guest speaker from a local medical lab technology college class (either an instructor or current student) or from a local lab and ask them to bring a centrifuge. In addition, a nephrologist would be a great guest speaker.

For a hands-on opportunity, take a field trip to a local lab to learn more about career opportunities in the lab and ask them to prepare several different slides for the students to see.

ADD A TWIST:

Add different urine tests such as Procedure 20.22: Using Reagent Strips to Test Urine or Procedure 20.23: Measuring Specific Gravity with Urinometer.

Change the patient to a female—Procedure20.26: Midstream Clean-Catch Urine, Female.

You knock on Mrs. Jones' door before you go back in. Mrs. Jones is a pretty independent and somewhat bossy 43-year-old woman. You have already helped her with some of her AM care, but she still needs to have an enema and a moist hot soak for her knee before she showers for the day.

Mrs. Jones tells you that she is actually looking forward to the enema, though she quickly clarifies—the results of the enema, not the actual administration! She tells you the iron pills the doctor has her on for her anemia have caused her major problems with constipation. Mrs. Jones said she needs to have a bowel movement before her visitors arrive at lunch time, so she will not be passing so much flatus and feeling so uncomfortable.

You explain to Mrs. Jones that you will be administering the moist hot soak for the osteoarthritis in her right knee first. You explain this will enable her right knee to bend more easily as she will need to have it bent for the enema procedure. After you complete this task, she comments on how much better her knee feels. She says she cannot wait for her abdomen to feel as good!

You explain the oil retention enema procedure to Mrs. Jones and instruct her that she will need to stay on her side and try to retain the enema solution for about 30 minutes. After administering the enema you tell her you will be checking on her every few minutes.

Twenty-five minutes later Mrs. Jones tells you it is time—she cannot hold it any longer. You assist her to the bathroom. She also announces that she will take a shower right after having her bowel movement and please be sure her new gown and towels are in the bathroom. You know you should not get annoyed, and you try to put yourself in Mrs. Jones' place. You know that she must be scared and feel out of control; she is waiting to get her test results back and has not seen the doctor yet today.

While Mrs. Jones is out of the bed, you make her bed, make sure her water pitcher is full, and move on to your next patient.

QUESTIONS TO ANSWER:

- Why would a moist hot soak be used for osteoarthritis?
- Why is the Sims' position used for enema administration?
- What would you do if the patient could not retain the enema for the needed time?
- How can you handle dealing with a patient that is overly demanding and unreasonable?

INSTRUCTOR NOTES:

The following procedures are pertinent for this scenario:

Procedure	Equipment Needed
20.17: Left Sims' Position	Bed
18.67: Oil Retention Enema	Prepackaged oil retention enema
	Bedpan and cover
	Waterproof bed protector
	Toilet tissue
	Towel, basin of water, and soap
	Disposable gloves
19.1: Preparing Moist Hot Soaks	Moist heat hot pads
	Towel
18.23: Assisting to the Bathroom	Slippers
	Robe
18.57: Making an Open Bed	Disposable gloves
	Draw sheet or large pad
	Two sheets or fitted bottom sheet and one large sheet
	Pillowcase
	Blankets as needed
	Bedspread (if a clean one is needed)
	Pillow
18.63: Providing Fresh Drinking Water	Water pitcher
	Cup

TEACHING TIPS/STRATEGIES:

Make sure the student is assessing the skin every 5 minutes when the moist hot soak is applied. Ask them to explain how this treatment is beneficial (i.e., heat decreases stiffness in tendons and ligaments).

Discuss with students what other applications there are for a moist hot soak.

The enema demonstration or simulation needs to done on a model, not a real person. Standard precautions and patient privacy are of utmost importance while administering an enema. Proper body mechanics must also be maintained.

Make sure the student ensures that the wheels on the bed are locked before raising the bed to appropriate height when turning the patient and administering the enema.

Be sure the student lowers the bed after giving the enema and puts the call bell in reach. The student needs to check on the patient every 5 minutes.

Discuss with students the possible problems that can result for patients straining to have a bowel movement.

Discuss with students the methods that are used to try to prevent constipation.

Faded Photographs

You have been working as a recreational therapist in a long-term care facility for about three years. Today you will be working with residents in the Alzheimer's Unit, a job that can be quite trying sometimes but also quite rewarding.

Today, you hope the music therapy and art therapy sessions you have planned will help them recall multiple memories. You have planned a music therapy session from 9:00 to 10:00 this morning, followed by an art therapy session from 10:00 to 11:00.

Billy Bancroft is one of the residents who will be attending your sessions today. Billy is 84 years old, but if you ask him his age, he will swear he is 32. Billy was a drummer in a band when he was in his twenties and thirties.

Matilda Owens, 90 years old, will also be attending your session. Matilda is new to the facility. She claims to be 39 and believes she is still teaching first grade at a local elementary school. She is constantly asking when her students will be finished with their physical education class.

The final resident that will attend your sessions today is Henrietta Haywood. Henrietta believes she is 21 and a dancer for the USO that boosts morale for the American Armed forces. When you check her records, you discover that she is really 79 years old and she did dance for the USO for twelve years.

As you enter the recreation area, you see Mr. Bancroft and Ms. Haywood sitting in front of the television, which is turned to a popular game show. Ms. Owens is pacing the room trying to find her students.

QUESTIONS TO ANSWER:

- Considering your patients' ages and interests, what type of music selections will you choose for their music therapy?

- Why can Ms. Haywood not remember how to brush her teeth, but still remember all the dance steps she learned?

- How might art therapy help Alzheimer patients recall memories?

- How will you handle a resident who does not want to cooperate and participate in the therapy session?

INSTRUCTOR NOTES:

In this scenario, students have the opportunity to perform the following procedures:

Procedure	Equipment Needed
15.1: Activities with Alzheimer's Patients	See Procedures 15.2 and 15.3
15.2: Music Therapy	Multiple music selections from different time eras
	Musical instruments
	Pictures that mean something to the patient
15.3: Art Therapy	Nontoxic acrylic paints or watercolor paints
	Paint brushes and canvases or watercolor paper
	Clay
	Colored pencils

TEACHING TIPS/STRATEGIES:

Have various music selections available from the 40s, 50s, 60s, 70s, 80s, 90s, and current hits. Students should determine that patients think they are in the 50s and select music from this time period. This can be determined by subtracting how old the person thinks they are from their actual age—i.e., Billy is 84 (actual age) minus 32 (the age Billy thinks he is) equals 52 years; then subtract this number from the current year. Discuss why music selection is important.

Have a wide selection of art supplies available for students to choose from. Include some sharp objects (such as scissors) and tools that they should not use because of safety issues. Discuss why these would not be appropriate for Alzheimer's patients.

Invite a speaker from the Alzheimer's Association and/or a therapist that works with Alzheimer's patients to provide strategies for working with these residents.

Discuss which professional characteristics would be used when working with patients with dementia as well as strategies for dealing with noncompliant patients.

An extension of this procedure into the community would include having students plan and carry out an art therapy session or music therapy session at a local long-term care facility.

33 | I Can Do It Myself!

While in anesthesia training, you are working part-time as a nurse at a small local hospital. Today you have been assigned to work on a medical unit where many of the patients have chronic medical conditions, such as cardiac or renal problems.

As you enter your first patient's room, you are greeted with a pleasant, "Good Morning!" You are pleased to make the acquaintance of Doug Munroe. Doug is a 58-year-old male who has been recently diagnosed with Parkinson's Disease. Doug has some minor tremors, but with just a small amount of assistance, he can get out of bed and ambulate around the room. He is very independent and wants to care for himself as much as possible.

The first order of business is to assist Mr. Munroe in getting ready for breakfast. You search for his toothbrush and toothpaste so he can brush his teeth when he goes into the bathroom to empty his bladder. Mr. Munroe is being evaluated for some kidney problems and is on a low-sodium diet. He has had some swelling in his lower extremities recently, so the doctors are running some diagnostic tests.

The aroma in the hall lets you know the breakfast carts have arrived. It smells like homemade cinnamon rolls today. You gather Mr. Munroe's tray and set him up for breakfast. He assures you he can feed himself, so you move on to your other patients.

While you are feeding Mrs. Patel down the hall, Mr. Munroe's doctor makes his rounds and writes the following orders:

Midstream clean-catch urine specimen today

24-hour urine test for creatinine

You gather the equipment and go in to help Mr. Munroe, who is uncircumcised, get started with his tests.

QUESTIONS TO ANSWER:

- What types of food should Mr. Munroe not be allowed to eat on a low sodium diet?
- What happens if you accidentally discard a urine specimen during the 24-hour period?
- When should you collect the midstream clean-catch urine specimen?
- Why is it important to encourage Mr. Munroe's independence? (Include both physical and psychological reasons.)

INSTRUCTOR NOTES:

In this scenario, students have the opportunity to perform the following procedures:

Procedure	Equipment Needed
17.1: Hand Hygiene (Washing)	Sink
	Soap
	Paper towels
	Trash can
	Nail brush (if available)
17.2: Personal Protective Equipment	Gloves
18.23: Assisting to the Bathroom	Gait belt
	Slippers
	Robe
18.17: Oral Hygiene—Ambulatory Patient	Toothbrush
	Toothpaste
	Towel
	Glass
18.62: Serving Food to Patient in Bed (Self-Help)	Several food trays with different diet cards
	Flex straws
	Towel
18.77: Midstream Clean-Catch Urine Male	Antiseptic solution or soap and water or towelettes
	Sterile specimen container tissues
	Disposable gloves
18.82: 24-Hour Urine Test	Special urine container
	Label for the container
	Specimen hat container or clean urinal
	Sign about urine collection
	Medical history
	Ice or other way to keep urine cool

TEACHING TIPS/STRATEGIES:

It is suggested that one student role plays the patient and one student role plays the nurse.

Have several different types of food trays prepared that represent different diets. Students need to remember to check for a low-sodium diet label. Also have things on the trays that need to be opened by the students, such as packages of silverware, milk or juice cartons, a muffin that needs to be buttered, salt and pepper packages, etc. Silverware packets and salt/pepper packets can be picked up at fast food restaurants.

Check with local laboratories or hospitals to see if they would donate urine containers for 24-hour urines or specimen containers. These can also be purchased from medical supply catalogs.

Make sure students instruct patients to discard the first urine specimen before starting the 24-hour urine test. They should instruct the client to use this specimen for their clean-catch urine specimen. If they do not do this, they will not be able to get the clean-catch specimen until the 24-hour urine test is completed.

Examine all labels to make sure they are complete.

Discuss what personal protective equipment and standard precautions might be needed to complete these tasks.

Have information about a 24-hour urine test for creatine available for the students. They should consult this information to discover if they need a preservative and if the specimen needs to be kept on ice.

Ask students to describe the psychological and physical benefits of encouraging the patients to be mobile and independent as long as possible.

ADD A TWIST:

Have Mr. Munroe either be unable to speak English or be deaf. Both of these conditions would require increased critical thinking skills related to communication of instructions.

34 | A Wild Night in the ER

You are working the second shift in the emergency room at a small community hospital. You do not mind working there on Wednesday nights as it is usually pretty quiet. Tonight though, the waiting room is packed and they just keep coming.

You have seen 16 patients, and they all have complained of the same symptoms: severe headache, severe vomiting, diarrhea, and abdominal cramps. The patients range in age from 5 to 36 and the only things they have in common is that they all were at the same amusement park earlier today and they all state that the symptoms came on very suddenly. You are afraid you might have an epidemic on your hands.

The emergency physician notifies the health department, and they ask him if diagnostic tests for Salmonella have been done. He instructs you to obtain a routine urine specimen and stool specimen from each of the patients. Once you have obtained the stool specimens, he tells you to test them for occult blood. He tells you to take all precautions because he is not sure what disease this is and it might be contagious.

QUESTIONS TO ANSWER:

- What personal protective equipment will you need and what standard precautions will you need to take?
- How will you protect the patient's confidentiality and privacy in a crowded emergency room that may only have curtains separating the patient's exam room?
- Why would you need to notify the health department?

INSTRUCTOR NOTES:

In this scenario, students have the opportunity to perform the following procedures:

Procedure	Equipment Needed
17.1: Hand Hygiene (Washing)	Sink
	Soap
	Paper towels
	Trash can
	Nail brush (if available)
17.2: Personal Protective Equipment	Gloves
	Gown
18.74: Collect Specimen Under Transmission-Based Precautions	Gloves
	Gown
	Specimen cups
18.75: Routine Urine Specimen	Bedpan or urinal
	Graduated cup
	Urine specimen container
	Label
	Paper bag
	Disposable nonsterile gloves
	Fake urine
18.80: Stool Specimen Collection	Stool specimen container with label
	Wooden tongue depressor
	Disposable gloves
	Bedpan and cover
	Fake stool specimen
18.81: Occult Blood Hematest	Hematest reagent filter paper
	Hematest reagent tablet
	Distilled water
	Tongue blade
	Disposable gloves

TEACHING TIPS/STRATEGIES:

Instructors can change the scenario by requesting the students obtain a midstream urine specimen if they desire this skill to be performed.

Standard precautions need to be followed when collecting the specimens and caring for these patients. Prior to beginning this scenario, ask students what precautions will be needed and what personal protective equipment should be worn or used.

Water with yellow food coloring makes great urine, as does apple juice. The student could give the patient an empty urinal or container, and the patient could return with a urinal or container that now contains the fake urine. You can also purchase simulated urine from medical or biological supply companies that can be tested for sugar, proteins, etc.

Simulated feces specimens can be made by mixing pizza dough with red, blue, and green food coloring and rolling it in cocoa. It can be baked to be firm or if you want it softer, warm in the microwave. Small 100 Grand bars melted slightly make great feces also.

To ensure accurate results, make sure all specimens are labeled correctly.

In the emergency room, where patients are probably not in individual rooms, providing privacy and respecting patient confidentiality may be more of a challenge, but should be done. Discuss with students how they protect patient confidentiality in this situation.

This would be a great scenario in which to invite a medical laboratory technician or an epidemiologist to be a guest speaker and work through the scenario with the class.

Another extension of this activity would be to have students research Salmonella and indicate what results from the diagnostic tests would prove positive for this disease.

Multiple students could take on the role of patients; students could investigate what they all have in common. A good solution might be that they all purchased refreshments from a particular stand at the amusement park or they all ate at a chain restaurant right outside the park. Students would have to use investigative questioning to determine the common thread.

Have students problem solve; once they determine it is a Salmonella outbreak, what should happen next to these patients and how will they handle the crowd if more patients continue to come to the emergency room?

35 | Lie to Ride

Paul Pence is a 43-year-old male who has been admitted to your hospital with cancer of the liver. He has been undergoing chemotherapy and radiation treatments for the past week and has an IV and urinary catheter. Because his immune system is so weak from his treatments, he has been placed in protective isolation.

Today Paul has to go to the X-ray department for a cystoscopy with dye. He will need to be transported to radiology on a stretcher. You have been assigned this task and his procedure is scheduled for 0930.

Later in the morning, you receive word that Mr. Pence is finished with his procedure, and you need to report to radiology to pick him up. When you get to radiology, you find that he is still on a stretcher and still has an indwelling catheter. The radiologist tells you to plug the catheter when Mr. Pence returns to the room and then reconnect it in about 4 hours for 30 minutes. He wants to do this to help Mr. Pence with bladder retraining. After you disconnect the catheter, you have to measure the urine in the drainage bag and record it as Mr. Pence is on I&O.

QUESTIONS TO ANSWER:

- Are there any special precautions you need to take because Mr. Pence in on protective or reverse isolation?
- What role does body mechanics play in this scenario?
- How does plugging a catheter help with bladder retraining?

INSTRUCTOR NOTES:

In this scenario, students have the opportunity to perform the following procedures:

Procedure	Equipment Needed
17.1: Hand Hygiene (Washing)	Sink
	Soap
	Paper towels
	Trash can
	Nail brush (if available)
17.2: Personal Protective Equipment	Mask for patient
18.28: Transferring—Sliding from Bed to Gurney and Back	Gurney
	Cover sheet
	Coworker
18.30: Transferring—Moving a Patient on a Gurney or Stretcher	Gurney with patient on it

Procedure	Equipment Needed
18.70: Disconnecting an Indwelling Catheter	Disinfectant such as alcohol swabs or betadine swabs
	Sterile gauze sponges
	Sterile cap or plug
	Disposable gloves
18.73: Emptying the Urinary Drainage Bag	Graduated or measuring cup
	Disposable gloves
	Paper towel
	Alcohol swab
	Fake urine
18.66: Measuring Urinary Output	Bedpan, urinal
	Special container
	Graduate or measuring cup
	Disposable nonsterile gloves
	I&O sheet

TEACHING TIPS/STRATEGIES:

Three students will be needed for this scenario—two students to transport and one student to be the patient who has to be moved to the stretcher.

Safety and body mechanics are major issues with this scenario. Wheels on the gurney and the bed must be locked. The bed must be raised to the height of the gurney. Students must be positioned correctly so they can hold onto the draw sheet at the head and hips. Make sure that students secure the patient on the stretcher immediately with straps or side rails. Review these tips with students before they carry out this scenario.

The patient is on protective or reverse isolation. Students must use critical thinking skills to determine that they need to wear masks in the patient's room and that the patient needs to wear a mask when he leaves the room.

Water tinted with yellow food coloring can be used to simulate urine and is not sticky like apple juice can be. Simulated urine can also be purchased from medical supply companies. Put imitation urine in the catheter drainage bag so the student will have to empty it and determine the output. Change the amount each time so each student can be checked on the accuracy of their measurements.

While inserting the sterile plug in the end of the catheter, make sure the student does not allow the catheter tubing to touch anything. Discuss with the student why it is so important to prevent contamination of the tubing.

36 | Sweet Dreams Anita

When you report to work for the 3–11 shift at Sweet Pines Estate, you are told in report that Anita Huggins is failing fast and the doctors do not expect her to live through the night.

She had been talking to her husband, Hubert, earlier that day and he had died 10 years ago. Her kidneys are failing and she is having increased periods of Cheyne-Stokes breathing. Her blood pressure has been dropping also.

Her family had been called that morning and most were by her bedside or in the waiting area, but Anita did not seem to be aware they were there. Hospice has been working with the family for a while, so they were prepared to say good-bye. Anita's living will states she is a DNR.

Anita shares a semi-private room with her roommate Mazel Murdock. Mazel was very upset when you made rounds and did not want to be in the room alone if Anita died. They have become very close in the two years they have shared living space.

About 9:00 that night, Anita quietly passed away. Her family stayed with her for about another hour and then went home after telling you which funeral home they would be using. Once they left, you and your coworker began postmortem care.

QUESTIONS TO ANSWER:

- How can you help Mazel during the time Anita is dying?
- Why is it important to get dentures in the mouth right after the patient passes away?
- How would this scenario have been different if the patient did not have a living will and was not a DNR?
- What is your responsibility related to the patient's belongings?

INSTRUCTOR NOTES:

In this scenario, students have the opportunity to perform the following procedure:

Procedure	Equipment Needed
18.54: Postmortem Care	Wash basin with warm water
	Washcloth and towel
	Shroud/postmortem set
	Gurney or morgue cart
	Nonsterile disposable gloves

TEACHING TIPS/STRATEGIES:

Invite a representative from hospice or a local funeral home to speak to the class about death and dying.

Discuss the need for respectful patient care after death as well as in life.

Most of the students have never seen or touched a person that is dead. Allow students to express their feelings about death and their fears of working with a patient who has died.

Make sure identification tags are filled out correctly and attached appropriately.

Demonstrate how to apply shrouds before asking students to do this.

ADD A TWIST:

The patient does not have a living will and is not a DNR. Procedures that could be implemented:

- Procedure 21.2: Rescue Breathing—Adult

  and/or

- Procedure 21.22: Cardiopulmonary Resuscitation—Adult

Have the patient be from a culture or religion that has specific rituals that need to be carried out right before or right after death.

37 The Final Rodeo

As a child, little Joe Carter had always watched westerns with his father and dreamed of becoming a cowboy. Years later, he was living out his fantasy by working as a cowboy on a ranch in Oklahoma and competing in rodeos. Then, tragedy struck.

Four months ago, he was involved in a rodeo accident that left him paralyzed from the neck down. Being only 27 years old, this has been a major adjustment for him. He had to give up the career he had always dreamed of, move back in with his parents, and depend on someone else for every activity of daily living. Needless to say, Joe has been very depressed.

You have been assigned to be Joe's home-health aide. Five days a week, you come to Joe's house and help him with things such as hygiene, skin care, and meals. You are about the same age as Joe, and the two of you have become good friends. He really looks forward to your visits. Mr. and Mrs. Carter have put a hospital bed in Joe's room and gotten some other medical equipment, such as a wheelchair and mechanical lift.

Today you have several tasks you need to accomplish. First you need to get a weekly weight for Joe. Since he cannot stand, you will have to do this with a mechanical lift. During the night, Joe has slipped to the bottom of the bed. You will need to move him up in bed before you can use the lift.

Next, you must complete the basic tasks such as brushing his teeth and feeding him breakfast. You bathe Joe every other day and this was done yesterday, so you do not need to worry about a bath today. When you bathed him yesterday, you noticed a reddened area on his sacrum and you are worried about his skin breaking down and a decubitus forming.

Today you are going to position him on his right and then his left side for about two hours each and try to keep him off his back as much as possible. You will have to plan some things to entertain Joe when you turn him on his right side toward you. When he lies on his left side (away from you) he can watch television. Before you position him however, you want to do foot care on Joe and put on a new external urinary catheter. His toenails look like weapons.

When you get to Joe's home you get one more surprise. Due to his immobility and lack of feeling, constipation has become a problem for Joe. He has not had a bowel movement in five days and his abdomen is distended. You will have to add a packaged enema to the day's activities. You have a full day planned, so you better get started.

QUESTIONS TO ANSWER:

- Why would skin assessment be a major component of Joe's care?
- What extra challenges would you have administering an enema to a patient that is paralyzed?
- What resources could you use or recommend to the family to help deal with the patient's psychological health?
- What fears might a patient have about being lifted with a mechanical lift?

INSTRUCTOR NOTES:

In this scenario, students have the opportunity to perform the following procedures:

Procedure	Equipment Needed
17.1: Hand Hygiene (Washing)	Sink
	Soap
	Paper towels
	Trash can
	Nail brush (if available)
18.32: Helping the Helpless Patient to Move Up in Bed	2 people
20.4: Measuring Weight on a Mechanical Lift	Mechanical lift
	Sling
	Clean sheet
18.16: Oral Hygiene—Brushing the Patient's Teeth	Toothbrush
	Toothpaste
	Mouthwash
	Cup of water with straw
	Emesis basin
	Bath towel
	Tissues
	Disposable nonsterile gloves
18.64: Feeding the Helpless Patient	Food tray
	Several napkins
18.68: Prepackaged Enemas	Prepackaged enema
	Bedpan and cover
	Waterproof bed protector
	Toilet tissue
	Towel
	Basin of water
	Soap
	Disposable gloves

Procedure	Equipment Needed
18.52: Foot Care	Bath basin
	Warm water
	Bath thermometer
	Mild soap
	Towel
	Lotion
	Nail file
	Clean socks
18.72: External Urinary Catheter	Basin of warm water
	Bath thermometer
	Washcloth
	Towel
	Bath blanket
	Tincture of Benzoin spray
	Waterproof bed protector
	Gloves
	Plastic bag
	Condom with drainage tip
	Paper towel
	Urinary drainage bag
	Model of male genitalia
18.37: Turning Patient Toward You	Several pillows
18.35: Turning Patient Away from You	Several pillows

TEACHING TIPS/STRATEGIES:

Discuss the role body mechanics and safety will play in these skills. Make sure the student locks the wheels on the bed before using the lift and turning the patient/client. The student needs to raise the bed to the appropriate height when turning or moving the patient, brushing teeth, and applying the external catheter. Make sure bed is lowered at the conclusion of these procedures.

Make sure students find another person to help them when moving the helpless patient up in bed and when doing the mechanical lift.

Demonstrate how the mechanical lift scale is used before the students practice with it. The scale on the mechanical lift must be on zero before weighing the patient. If you do not have one in your classroom, ask a local long-term care facility to do an in-service for your class. Discuss with students how they can straighten wrinkles in the bed while the patient is up in the lift. This will help with skin care.

The student should experience what it feels like to sit in the mechanical lift. This will better prepare them to communicate with their patients/clients and help alleviate their fears.

Have a student role-play being the patient and another student role-play being the home-health aide. Have them use real toothpaste and mouthwash when brushing the teeth, so they can experience what it is like to be dependent on someone else for this basic hygiene task.

Have a food tray with real food available that has to be fed to the patient. This could include puddings, soups, muffins, ham, chicken, etc. It needs to include food that has to be seasoned and liquids for the patient/client to drink.

The patient is depressed, so the student playing this role can refuse to eat. The student playing the role of the home-health aide would need to encourage them to eat.

Fleet enemas can be purchased at a local pharmacy. Hospitals or pharmacies may donate enemas to you that are out of date. You can also purchase these from medical supply catalogs.

The enema demonstration or simulation needs to be done on a model, not a real person. Discuss what extra challenges there might be with administering an enema to a person that is paralyzed from the neck or waist down.

Discuss with the student what type of foot problems a person that is paralyzed might have.

Make sure the temperature of the water is checked when it is used for the "foot care" procedure and the "applying the external catheter" procedure.

A model of the male genitalia to which students apply an external urinary catheter will be needed.

Students need to note the condition of the penis when they remove the old external catheter and document this observation.

Students need to check catheter tubing after positioning the patient to make sure it is not kinked.

Discuss with students that addressing this patient's physical problems are only part of getting him well. Have them talk about what resources might be available to help with the patient's depression and life changes.

ADD A TWIST:

The patient/client could be on intake and output.

The patient/client could be on a therapeutic diet, such as diabetic or low cholesterol.

Irish Dancing on Hold

Patricia Quinlivan is a patient at Coastal Rehabilitation Center. Patricia had a knee replacement five days ago, and she has come to Coastal for additional physical and occupational therapy. Patricia is a widow and lives alone except for two cats, so her doctor felt a couple weeks in rehab would be the best thing for her.

Besides her knee issues, Patricia has been having some trouble with kidney stones. She had a lithotripsy procedure before leaving the hospital. The physician's discharge orders included straining her urine for renal calculi and checking each urine specimen for blood.

As you enter Mrs. Quinlivan's room, she is awake and wishes you a "top of the morning." You just love her Irish accent. She tells you that her "bladder is about to burst and could you please help her get on the bedside commode." She finds this more comfortable than the toilet because it is higher, and it is easier for her to get up and down. Once she finishes, you put down the lid on the bedside commode and help her back to bed.

Next on the agenda is getting a bath before breakfast and therapy. You prepare a bath basin for her to do a partial bath. Mrs. Quinlivan can do most of her bath, but she is just a wee bit stout. She will need some assistance cleaning her back and perineal area.

While she starts on her bath, you test her urine for blood and strain it. It is negative for blood and no evidence of kidney stones. By this time, Mrs. Quinlivan has done all of the bath she can manage. You change the water and then do her back and perineal care.

While Mrs. Quinlivan gets dressed in her favorite sweatsuit, you empty the bath basin and tidy up the room. Mrs. Quinlivan is in her wheelchair and ready for breakfast. She is anxious to get to the dining room to have her morning cup of coffee and chat with her new friends, Irma and Dorothy. You wheel her to the dining room and help her prepare for breakfast. Mrs. Quinlivan is on a regular diet, so she does not have any restrictions. After breakfast, she will be going to her physical therapy session.

Later that morning, you pick up Mrs. Quinlivan from therapy. She has worked really hard this morning and her knee is quite swollen. The therapist suggests that she return to her room and elevate it until lunch. She also tells you to apply a cold compress to her knee.

QUESTIONS TO ANSWER:

- It would be faster for you to give Mrs. Quinlivan a bedpan, rather than helping her up to the bedside commode. Why is it better for her to use the commode?

- What personal protective equipment will you need to carry out these procedures?

- How do you proceed if the HemaCombistix is positive for blood and/or you find stones or particles in the urine strainer?

INSTRUCTOR NOTES:

In this scenario, students have the opportunity to perform the following procedures:

Procedure	Equipment Needed
18.22: Elimination—Bedside Commode	Bedside commode
	Toilet tissue
	Washcloth
	Warm water
	Soap
	Towel
	Disposable nonsterile gloves
	Slippers
18.44: Giving a partial Bath (Face, Hands, Axillae, Buttocks, and Genitals)	Soap and soap dish
	Face towel
	Bath towel
	Washcloth
	Hospital gown or patient's sleepwear
	Lotion or powder
	Nail brush and emery board
	Comb and brush
	Bedpan and cover
	Bath blanket
	Bath basin
	Bath thermometer
	Clean linen, as needed
	Disposable gloves
18.78: HemaCombistix	Fake urine
	Bottle of HemaCombistix
	Nonsterile gloves

Procedure	Equipment Needed
18.79: Straining Urine	Fake urine
	Paper strainers or gauze
	Specimen container and label
	Laboratory request for analysis of specimen
	Sign for patient's room or bathroom explaining that all urine must be strained
	Nonsterile gloves
18.47: Perineal Care	Bath blanket
	Bedpan and cover
	Basin
	Solution, water, or other if ordered
	Cotton balls
	Waterproof protector for bed
	Disposable gloves
	Perineal pad and belt if needed
18.60: Preparing the Patient to Eat in the Dining Room	Wheelchair
19.2: Moist Cryotherapy (Cold) Compresses	Cool, wet cloth
	Plastic cover
	Dry towel

TEACHING TIPS/STRATEGIES:

Safety issues need to be emphasized in this scenario. Wheels on the bed need to be locked as well as wheels on the bedside commode and the wheelchair. The bed needs to be raised during perineal care, but then lowered so the patent/client can get up without any added risk of falling.

Slippers or shoes should be worn by the patient when they are out of bed to prevent slipping and falling. The call bell needs to be placed near the patient when she is on the bedside commode and when she is doing the partial bath.

Discuss why it is important to check water temperature during the bath and also when is it important to change water.

Question the students about what they would do differently if they were doing perineal care on a male versus a female.

Before using HemaCombistixs, review with the students how to use them. Emphasize how to remove strips from the bottle and that it is important not to touch the reagent pads on the strips with their fingers. Also review that students must follow instructions on the bottle as far as the timing of the test and that the strip with urine on it should not touch the bottle.

You can purchase fake urine that will test positive for blood from medical supply catalogs. You can also get HemaCombistixs and urine strainers from these catalogs.

It is important to instruct the patient not to put toilet tissue in the urine specimen.

Any stones or particles should be placed in a specimen container and the container should be labeled with the patient's name, room number, date, and time. These should be saved for the doctor to see and the specimen collection should be recorded on the progress notes.

Have students brainstorm about which personal protective equipment they will need to wear and use to complete these procedures.

When applying the cold compress, make sure you apply a plastic cover around the compress so the bed does not become wet.

Skin around the site should be checked frequently and the condition of skin documented.

ADD A TWIST:

The patient/client can be on I&O.

The HemaCombistix test could be positive and the students could have particles when they strain the urine.

The Magic Book

You are working as a pharmacy technician at a local drugstore. Jeanette McGregor, one of your regular customers, comes in and asks if you can give her some information about a drug her mother has recently been put on.

Her mother has a mild form of dementia and had taken all of her pills out of the bottles, put them in a jewelry box, and then threw away the bottles. Now her mother cannot remember what the name of the new medication is and what it is for.

You reach for the *Physicians' Desk Reference (PDR)* and tell her you will be happy to try and help. Mrs. McGregor shows your mother's new pill. It is a small, pink, round pill with a 200 on it. On the back it says "Abbott Laboratories." You turn to Section 4 of the *PDR* to look at the medication pictures and see what the name of the medicine is. You recognize the pill to be _____.

Once you tell Mrs. McGregor the name of the medication, she asks you what are the indications and usage for this particular medication. She was not sure why the doctor had prescribed it, as she had not been able to go with her mother to that appointment.

You turn to the "Brand and Generic Name Index" to see what page the product information for this drug would be on. You make a note that you need to turn to page _____, which is in the "Product Information" section.

When you turn to the "Product Information" section, you look for "Indications and Usage." You tell Mrs. McGregor that there are two reasons that this medication is given. They are:

1. _____

2. _____

You suggest that she check with her mother's physician to find out the particular reason he has prescribed this medication.

Mrs. McGregor thanks you for your help and asks if she can just take up a few more minutes of your time. As long as you have the *PDR* handy, she wonders what the usual dose is and if there are any general adverse reactions she needs to be on the lookout for with her mother. You research this for her and write down the information on a pharmacy notepad (see following page).

Pharmacy R$_X$ Notepad

Name of Drug: _____

Usual Dose: _____

General Adverse Reactions:

1. _____   4. _____

2. _____   5. _____

3. _____   6. _____

After Mrs. McGregor leaves, you get a call from Nanette Nightingale. She is new to the state and is trying to update her emergency numbers. She asks if you could please give her the name and phone number for the Poison Control Center in this state.

Once again, you open your *PDR* and turn to Section 3 where all the state Poison Control Centers are listed. You give the phone number and address for the one in this state. She is very grateful.

Your final phone call for the morning is from a physician's assistant. He has a patient with severe diarrhea, and he wants to know what the best medications are for this problem. He is on call and does not have his *PDR* at home. He knew you would have access to one.

You tell him you will be happy to tell him what is listed in the *PDR*. You turn to the "Product Category Index" section and look under "Antidiarrheals Medications." You tell him the first three medications listed.

1. _____

2. _____

3. _____

Before disconnecting, he asks you to do him one more favor. He needs to get some more Lanoxin samples for his office and wants to talk to the manufacturer about this. He knows they are made by GlaxoSmithKline. He asks you if you could give him their phone number and address so he can contact them. You tell him no problem, and turn to the "Manufacturers' Index" in your *PDR*.

The phone number is _____ and the address is

_____.

You look at your watch and notice it is 11:30 and almost time for lunch. It has been a busy morning, and the time has flown. Thank goodness for your trusty *PDR*.

INSTRUCTOR NOTES:

In this scenario, students have the opportunity to perform the following procedure:

Procedure	Equipment Needed
20.20: Using the *Physicians' Desk Reference (PDR)*	PDR

TEACHING TIPS/STRATEGIES:

New editions of the *PDR* are published each year. Check with your local pharmacies and physician offices to see if they might donate old copies of the *PDR* to your classroom. You can also purchase the new edition from bookstores and online.

The colors of the pages of the sections do change. Instruct your students to learn the names of the sections and not memorize the colors of the pages.

Another activity would be to have students find out the name of a medication that a family member was on and have them research it in the *PDR*. They could make a drug information card.

Following, you will find the scenario with answers.

ANSWERS: "THE MAGIC BOOK"

You are working as a pharmacy technician at a local drugstore. Jeanette McGregor, one of your regular customers, comes in and asks if you can give her some information about a drug her mother has recently been put on.

Her mother has a mild form of dementia and had taken all of her pills out of the bottles, put them in a jewelry box, and then threw away the bottles. Now her mother cannot remember what the name of the new medication is and what it is for.

You reach for the *Physicians' Desk Reference (PDR)* and tell her you will be happy to try and help. Mrs. McGregor shows your mother's new pill. It is a small, pink, round pill with a 200 on it. On the back it says "Abbott Laboratories." You turn to Section 4 of the *PDR* to look at the medication pictures and see what the name of the medicine is. You recognize the pill to be __Synthroid 200 mcg__.

Once you tell Mrs. McGregor the name of the medication, she asks you what are the indications and usage for this particular medication. She was not sure why the doctor had prescribed it, as she had not been able to go with her mother to that appointment.

You turn to the "Brand and Generic Name Index" to see what page the product information for this drug would be on. You make a note that you need to turn to page (this will vary depending on the year the PDR was published), which is in the "Product Information" section.

When you turn to the "Product Information" section, you look for "Indications and Usage." You tell Mrs. McGregor that there are two reasons that this medication is given. They are:

1. ___Hypothyrodism___

2. ___Pituitary TSH Suppression___

You suggest that she check with her mother's physician to find out the particular reason he has prescribed this medication.

Mrs. McGregor thanks you for your help and asks if she can just take up a few more minutes of your time. As long as you have the *PDR* handy, she wonders what the usual dose is and if there are any general adverse reactions she needs to be on the lookout for with her mother. You research this for her and write down the information on a pharmacy notepad (see below).

Pharmacy R$_X$ Notepad

Name of Drug: _____ Synthroid 200 mcg _____

Usual Dose: __One daily ½–1 hour before breakfast__

General Adverse Reactions:

1. __Fatigue__	4. __Heat Intolerance__
2. __Increased Appetite__	5. __Fever__
3. __Weight Loss__	6. __Excessive Sweating__

After Mrs. McGregor leaves, you get a call from Nanette Nightingale. She is new to the state and is trying to update her emergency numbers. She asks if you could please give her the name and phone number for the Poison Control Center in this state.

Once again, you open your *PDR* and turn to Section 3 where all the state Poison Control Centers are listed. You give the phone number and address for the one in this state. She is very grateful.

Your final phone call for the morning is from a physician's assistant. He has a patient with severe diarrhea, and he wants to know what the best medications are for this problem. He is on call and does not have his *PDR* at home. He knew you would have access to one.

You tell him you will be happy to tell him what is listed in the *PDR*. You turn to the "Product Category Index" section and look under "Antidiarrheals Medications." You tell him the first three medications listed.

1.   Imodium A-D Liquid, Caplets and E-Z Chew

2.   Imodium Advanced Caplets and Chewable Tablets

3.   Lotronex Tablets

Before disconnecting, he asks you to do him one more favor. He needs to get some more Lanoxin samples for his office and wants to talk to the manufacturer about this. He knows they are made by GlaxoSmithKline. He asks you if you could give him their phone number and address so he can contact them. You tell him no problem, and turn to the "Manufacturers' Index" in your *PDR*.

The phone number is   919-483-2100   and the address is

   GlaxoSmith Kline, Five Moore Drive, Research Triangle Park, North Carolina, 27704   .

You look at your watch and notice it is 11:30 and almost time for lunch. It has been a busy morning, and the time has flown. Thank goodness for your trusty *PDR*.